MADE AT HOME
VEGETABLES

Thank you to everyone who has taken the time to teach us so that we can now pass it on to Indy and anyone else who will listen

Vegetables
by Dick & James Strawbridge

First published in Great Britain in 2012
by Mitchell Beazley, an imprint of Octopus
Publishing Group Limited, Endeavour House,
189 Shaftesbury Avenue, London, WC2H 8JY
www.octopusbooks.co.uk

An Hachette UK Company
www.hachette.co.uk

ISBN: 978-1-84533-656-1

A CIP catalogue record for this book is
available from the British Library

Printed and bound in China

Neither the authors nor the publishers take
any responsibility for any injury or damage
resulting from the use of techniques shown or
described in this book.

Both metric and imperial measurements are given
for the recipes. Use one set of measures only,
not a mixture of both.

Standard level spoon measurements are used in
all recipes
1 tablespoon = 15ml
1 teaspoon = 5ml

Ovens should be preheated to the specified
temperature. If using a fan-assisted oven,
follow the manufacturer's instructions for
adjusting the time and temperature. Grills
should also be preheated.

This book includes dishes made with nuts and
nut derivatives. It is advisable for those
with known allergic reactions to nuts and nut
derivatives and those who may be potentially
vulnerable to these allergies, such as pregnant
and nursing mothers, invalids, the elderly,
babies and children to avoid dishes made with
nuts and nut oils.

It is also prudent to check the labels of
preprepared ingredients for the possible
inclusion of nut derivatives.

The Department of Health advises that eggs
should not be consumed raw. This book contains
some dishes made with raw or lightly cooked
eggs. It is prudent for more vulnerable people
such as pregnant and nursing mothers, invalids,
the elderly, babies and young children to avoid
uncooked or lightly cooked dishes made with eggs.

MADE AT HOME
DICK & JAMES STRAWBRIDGE

VEGETABLES

MITCHELL BEAZLEY

CONTENTS

INTRODUCTION

We didn't start growing our own vegetables to help reduce our impact on the environment, nor did we first plant a row of salads to save money. In fact, we started growing vegetables at home because we enjoyed it. Spending time with family outside and digging the earth to sow seeds is a special experience: you can learn from previous generations of gardeners and then add your own take on this shared knowledge. We love to blend traditional techniques with more modern growing methods.

However, these days our main motivation for weeding outside in hot weather or earthing up rows of spuds in the rain is that we both love to cook. Vegetables you have grown yourself always taste better than anything that you can buy in the shops. Some households maintain a clear distinction between inside and outside, but for us, the move from the garden to the kitchen is often seamless -- vegetables come straight inside after harvesting and are swiftly presented on a plate. This unbroken chain from seed to plated meal allows you to have total control of the food you eat.

LEARNING
Growing your own food can be a daunting prospect to the first-time gardener, as there are lots of elements you need to master. There is a whole new vocabulary to learn, complete with localized jargon, as well as a variety of approaches, techniques and contradictory advice to absorb. Our attitude is that anyone can grow vegetables, so don't worry about it -- as you follow the basic suggestions in this book, you can't go far wrong.

By growing your own food you can cut down on food miles, provide healthy ingredients for cooking and -- without sounding too hippy about it -- feed the soul. You will learn along the way -- mistakes that self-confessed 'gardening virgins' often find themselves faced with include accidentally growing hundreds of courgettes, going away on holiday and forgetting to arrange for someone to water your plants and losing your cabbages to caterpillars because you didn't protect them with netting. The good thing is that each challenge you deal with results in you becoming a more experienced kitchen gardener. And don't forget, you are not alone -- there are lots of other gardeners out there.

SOWING & GROWING

When it comes to choosing your seeds, it makes sense to start with those vegetables that you enjoy and which are well suited to the area you live in. We steer clear of 'F1 Hybrid' seeds, as they are bred to be used only once, and the seeds of the plants cannot be saved and used the following year. Non-hybrid and heirloom varieties allow you to produce generations of plants from a single packet of seeds. Approach growing with an open mind: try anything once, but remember that if it goes wrong, the first time can be an accident, the second a mistake and the third time enemy action; so learn from what you are doing. If a particular plant doesn't work for you, try an alternative.

The soil or compost you grow your food in is obviously important, and it is to be nurtured and cherished. Compost can be expensive and bulky to buy so why not make your own? When preparing vegetables, we always keep an empty colander next to the chopping board and throw in any peelings, roots, tops or pips as we go along. Not only does it help us keep our work area tidy while we are cooking, it also means nothing goes to waste. After some time in a compost bin, these scraps will be providing the nutrients for next year's goodies. Composting is an art that you'll learn to enjoy.

The growing period is a time to enjoy the transformation from seed to seedling to plant to abundant harvest. Your charges will not require constant attention -- intervening when required is what matters. A bit of weeding (we like using a hoe) at the right time is enough to give your plants the advantage they need.

SEASONALITY

The time it takes for your vegetables to grow and mature means that you learn patience as a gardener. You will experience the changing seasons, and it won't take long for you to realize how special the relatively short period is when your vegetables are ready for harvest. Garden chefs soon come to know what can be savoured at any given time, because every time you walk around your garden you will get an indication of what is ready to harvest. It is in this way that you will become reconnected with the seasons and start looking forward to certain times of the year because of what is on offer in the garden. Use this knowledge to give you a perspective when buying other local produce. We hardly ever buy out-of-season vegetables now, as they just don't compare to our home-grown seasonal crops.

ENJOYING THE HARVEST

Harvesting is the reason we grow our produce. The temptation to harvest early will be overwhelming, but experience will allow you to determine when produce is at its best. Larger not only means more mature, it also tends to mean more flavour -- it's just that the texture of the vegetable can be tougher, too. It is up to you to figure out exactly how you like your produce -- and, of course, the freshness will give you flavour that you just can't buy.

Once you have grown your own vegetables you will really start to appreciate cooking them. We find that after months or weeks of waiting, the cooking is a fantastic reward. You will find yourself thinking up more and more inventive recipes, as the act of putting your produce together in a dish becomes the culmination of all your hard work. This makes it all the more tasty! Too much pride can arguably be a bad thing, but when it comes to serving a dish made with 100% home-grown ingredients, you will be beaming.

STORAGE

If you have grown your own vegetables then you've probably gone through a long process -- sowing, transplanting, watering, weeding, harvesting. The last thing you are going to want to do is waste your fresh crop. You will soon find yourself exploring the best methods of storing them, and learning a variety of preserving techniques.

GETTING THE MOST FROM YOUR GARDEN

Some of the approaches covered in this book will be more applicable to your particular plot and lifestyle than others, but you can make a kitchen garden almost anywhere, to suit any set of circumstances -- don't let your busy schedule or small garden stop you from having a go. The key thing to remember is that you should aim to make the most productive use of your time and the space available. But above all, your aim will be to grow tasty food that you like to eat. Making your own kitchen garden is a satisfying and enjoyable experience -- done right, it makes you smile, fills you with pride and tastes good, too.

Dick & James

GROW VEGETABLES

In order to have a successful kitchen garden, you need to determine exactly what you are trying to achieve, by planning how much work you want or are able to do and how you will make the most of your plot. After planting it, you have to maintain your garden -- it will require regular watering and weeding. In order to maximize your harvest, it is also important to sustain productivity by feeding nutrients to your plants, encouraging beneficial insects to help with pollination and deterring pests. But above all, keep in mind that a kitchen garden is a great excuse for spending more time outside and proudly reaping the rewards of your hard work -- we hope that our gardening basics will help you get plenty of tasty vegetables on to your kitchen table.

TOOLS & EQUIPMENT

- Dibber – a pointed stick for making holes in the ground before sowing larger seeds.
- Fork, hoe and spade – the key tools required for growing vegetables, so invest in solid ones that will last. Sharpen your hoe once a year.
- Riddle – akin to a sieve, to remove stones and work the soil into a fine tilth perfect for covering small seeds.
- Seed trays – seed trays and growing modules are excellent for growing seedlings.
- Pots – keep a selection in all shapes and sizes (remember to put some bits of broken pots or stones in the bottom of larger pots to help with drainage).
- Cold frames and cloches – growing under cover is a highly effective gardening technique: you can extend the growing season and protect seedlings from frost and pests. You can make cold frames and cloches very cheaply.
- Propagator – useful for growing more delicate seeds or starting an early crop under cover.
- Raised beds – great for growing fruit and vegetables, and the added height makes gardening easier on your back.
- Compost bins – a double bin made out of old wooden pallets will provide good compost for your beds and keep a small plot looking tidy.
- Shed – a well-organized garden shed on your allotment will save you from carrying your tools and equipment to and fro every time.

SOIL PREPARATION

The foundation of a productive kitchen garden is the quality of the soil. Whatever the size your plot, be it a raised bed in an urban back garden or a large outdoor bed on a smallholding, your kitchen garden will thrive if you remember to keep on top of the weeding and add plenty of rich, nutritious organic matter to the soil. Your soil will be not only more productive, but also a pleasure to work with.

It takes a significant amount of work with a fork and a rake to achieve a fine, crumbly, stone-free soil, known as tilth, but it's worth it. Be patient and remember that soil fertility doesn't increase overnight. Experience has taught us that when it comes to boosting the vitality of our chosen crops, conditioning the soil is absolutely worthwhile (see pages 18–21).

CHOOSING WHAT TO PLANT

Choosing what to grow requires some careful thought. You may opt for high-yield crops or expensive luxury varieties, low-maintenance perennials or quick-growing cut-and-come-again crops. It is worth taking into account what you like to eat and how much it costs, but the bottom line is to have a go and enjoy it.

Alongside annual vegetables such as courgettes and tomatoes, we would suggest growing a variety of perennial vegetables such as wild rocket, perpetual spinach, globe and Jerusalem artichokes, asparagus and, of course, some herbs and horseradish. One of the great things about perennials is that they tend to require very little maintenance and are relatively hardy. Just remember that most varieties will need a bit of pruning at some point in the year to boost their growth.

Choosing what to grow is the first step, followed by where and only then how. Where and how to plant depends upon the particular crop you have chosen to grow, and there are specific amounts of moisture, nutrients, warmth and light that certain plants need in order to flourish – this will be covered later for each individual vegetable.

SEEDS

The initial energy a new plant will need to germinate and grow is stored in the seed. It's in your interest to look after your seeds well, so store them in a dark, dry place and handle them carefully when you eventually plant them.

Getting hold of seeds is relatively easy. You can either save some seeds from already growing heirloom vegetables in order to plant them or you can buy seeds from a catalogue or in a local garden centre. We tend to do a mix of the two. Saving seeds does take up extra time and storage space, but on the whole it is extremely satisfying and a much cheaper way of gardening. You follow the same process you would use for keeping seeds to cook with: pumpkin seeds, for example, are delicious and can be saved when you are cooking the rest of the vegetable. Simply scrape them out of the flesh, rub clean, place on kitchen paper and leave on the window sill until dry (they should be brittle and no longer bendy). Store pumpkin seeds in a jar in a dark cupboard before planting or eating. Make sure to sow your seeds at the right time and at the right depth. Place the seeds in the palm of one hand, gently pick some of them up with the thumb and forefinger of your other hand and sprinkle them carefully. If they are too small to handle, then mix them with

some sand to make sowing easier. Once sown, evenly cover the seeds with a little soil and give them a gentle watering in. Seeds need moisture to develop but it's important not to overdo it, as you don't want to end up flooding them. Seeds that are too wet can develop all sorts of problems and fungal diseases.

SOWING DIRECT INTO THE GROUND

Sowing direct into the ground in drills is the method we use with most of our root crops and some later crops – it cuts down the time required for transplanting. Plant when the ground is moist or when rain is forecast.

- Ensure the ground is finely raked and free of stones.
- Mark a row out with some string.
- Use a hoe or spade to dig a shallow drill and very thinly sprinkle the seeds straight into the ground (some crops

like peas and beans are better planted individually at regular intervals).
- Cover with soil and after 1–2 weeks 'thin out' the seedlings if they appear to be overcrowded so that they have more room to grow. Instead of just composting the unwanted plants, transplant any seedlings you have 'pricked out' into another seedbed or pot.
- Keep the spaces between the rows weed-free while the seedlings are in their early stages so that they don't get lost.

SOWING UNDER COVER & IN SEEDBEDS

Having the space to grow seedlings under cover or indoors is invaluable: in temperate regions, it allows you to start your growing season earlier and make the most of the short summers, while also providing your seedlings with a great initial boost and protection from frost and pests. Plus, when it's raining heavily and you can't face weeding outside, you will always somewhere warm and dry to be productive.

Propagators can provide extra heat for seeds to germinate and develop in a safe environment. You can buy electrically heated units but we find using simple gravel trays with lids or growing our seeds in trays and then covering with plastic tops to keep them warm very effective. However, the trays do take up quite a lot of space.
- Sow the seeds in a tray filled with potting compost or into small pots.
- The trays can dry out quickly on warm days, so make sure to water regularly.
- When the first seedlings appear, thin

accustom your plants to the cold before transplanting them out in the appropriate bed in the garden.

- Take plants outside on warmer days and bring them in at night until there is no risk of frost. Alternatively, if you are growing seedlings outside in a cold frame, leave the lid open during the day and close it at night.
- Make sure to plant your seedlings out at the right time: either when the pot is full of roots (this shows that the seedling has used up all the available nutrients in its limited space and is searching for more) or when the risk of frost has passed. If in doubt, be patient and wait that extra week — it's far too easy to be optimistic and regret it later when the plants suffer from an unexpected cold spell.

them out to allow them more room to grow.
- We often start seeds off in small pots and as the seedling grows strong and healthy, we transplant it to a larger pot before the plant goes outside into the bed.

Sowing in modules is another option: there is no need to thin out seedlings and no disturbance to the roots when it's time to transplant.

If you don't have a greenhouse or poly-tunnel, it's still worth designating one part of your plot as a seedbed for bringing on small plants in a weed-free area with a nice, fine tilth.

HARDENING OFF & TRANSPLANTING
It is important to harden off seedlings growing in trays under cover, so try to

SUCCESSION PLANTING
Succession planting is as simple as it sounds: by planting small amounts of the same crop every couple of weeks, you can assure a regular supply over the entire growing season, avoiding gluts of one type of crop, all fruiting at the same time.

WATERING
It is vital to keep your vegetables well watered at certain stages of their growth: they will be thirsty when you have just sown them, at transplanting and later when they are in flower. Water in the morning or evening to reduce surface evaporation.

Try to make the most of rainwater by installing water butts beneath guttering

Greater biodiversity in your garden is one of the cheapest and most effective tools for greater productivity – it will help with pollination of your vegetables, improve plant health and reduce time spent worrying about pest control. Consider designing appropriate habitats for insects that will hunt your pests and untamed areas that will attract a wide range of wildlife. For example, putting a small pond near your crops can encourage all sorts of beneficial insects and amphibians.

IMPROVING YOUR SOIL

Nurturing the soil is a bit like mixing together the right ingredients in a recipe and will directly determine how well your vegetables come out. We enrich our soil with calcified seaweed, green manures and animal manure, and have increasingly taken to making liquid fertilizers to boost the vitality of certain crops in the growing season. Composting accelerates the natural decomposition of organic matter to create rich soil to use around your plot. Given the right conditions, bacteria, fungi and micro-organisms will thrive and break down waste quickly, turning it into quality compost. Successfully making your own compost depends on getting the right balance of materials high in carbon and those high in nitrogen. An easy way to divide up these different types of materials is to categorize them as 'Greens' or 'Browns'.

Greens (high in Nitrogen)
- Grass cuttings
- Uncooked fruit and vegetable peelings
- Tea bags, coffee grounds

downpipes. A larger rainwater harvesting system may be a worthwhile investment if you want to grow lots of your own food or if your water is metered.

WEEDS

Weeds are the first plants to fill bare soil. Try to tackle weeds before they become a problem or go to seed. Use a sharp hoe and remove as many roots as possible. Hot composting or burning is the only way to kill some weed seeds.

PEST CONTROL

Scarecrows, beer traps, copper tape, netting and old CDs hanging in the wind are all good ways of keeping down pest problems. Look at individual plant profiles for advice about dealing with particular pests.

- Manure
- Urine
- Weeds
- Fresh plants
- Grass clippings

Browns (high in carbon)
- Straw
- Dead leaves
- Cardboard
- Shredded paper
- Loo rolls, cardboard
- Egg cartons
- Twigs, plant stems and prunings
- Sawdust, wood chippings

Aim for between 25 and 50% Greens. The right mix of soft Greens and woody, dry Browns will mean that air can still circulate around the material, preventing your compost heap from becoming wet and smelly.

COOL COMPOSTING
Cool composters are probably the most common style of compost bin. Due to their small size, they do not retain much heat but instead encourage a large worm population. Worms are the stars of the compost world, working alongside the micro-organsims to break down materials and aerate the soil. With cool composting, you need to add small amounts of waste to the bin regularly – remember to add equal amounts of wet and dry material to stop it from becoming smelly. These types of lidded compost bin are very easy and produce a good-quality compost, but we would recommend emptying them out every couple of months and 'turning' the compost before putting it back in – this means getting it all out on the floor and using a fork to mix it up. Turning is a great opportunity to see if you need

to add more or less of any particular material to your compost: if it looks too wet add more Browns, and if it is too dry and fibrous then add more Greens.

HOT COMPOSTING
The advantages of hot composting are that the process kills weed seeds and diseases and reduces pathogens. We have built a few large hot-composting systems using old wooden pallets, which can often be found for free. Knock them together into 2 adjoining wooden boxes, each about 1 cubic metre (about 35 cubic feet) in size. The wood helps retain the heat created by the composting process. For extra insulation, line the insides of the boxes with cardboard and plug the gaps between the planks with bubble wrap. If you are processing large quantities of material, it may be worth using a shredder to cut some of it up before adding it to the heap. Cover the heap with black plastic or a piece of old carpet to help retain the high temperatures.

Turning the compost heap every month with a fork – moving it from one box to the other, while making sure you get the material on the outside to the inside and visa versa – will add air and keep the heat up significantly. This style of composting allows you to keep an eye on the progress of the mixture as you turn it – make sure to keep the heap moist in dry weather. The compost will take between 6 months and 2 years to mature.

ANAEROBIC COMPOSTING
Some organic materials are harder to compost: cooked food, meat, fish and dairy tend to putrefy and rot, producing strong smells, and will attract rats and vermin to your compost bin. One option is to try out an anaerobic digester or Green Cone – a type of waste digester consisting of a basket that sits below the ground and is covered with a plastic cone. When food waste is added to the digester, it rots down inside the cone and the nutrients leak into the surrounding soil. The other option for safely disposing of cooked food instead of putting it into landfill is to use Bokashi – a bran-like substance made up of effective micro-organisms – as a form of anaerobic composting. The process depends on an odourless, airtight container, in which the micro-organisms ferment and break down food waste so that it can be added to a conventional compost bin without the risk of attracting rats. The other by-product is an incredibly strong liquid fertilizer that can be diluted with water for feeding plants in the garden.

WORMERIES
In an urban environment we would recommend a wormery as the first choice for composting, as it requires so little space. You can build your own wormery or buy ones that stack in vertical tiers to save space. The other main attraction of a wormery is the amazing liquid fertilizer, or 'worm tea', that collects at the base and is rocket fuel for garden plants.

LEAF MOULD
Leaf mould is an great way of making your own compost to use as a soil conditioner or for potting. All you need to do it collect fallen leaves and put them into black plastic bags that you have made

build a large cage with 4 wooden posts and some chicken wire and shred the leaves before putting them into the leaf-bin. Another option is to collect leaves using a lawn mower as it chops them up and mixes them with grass, which is high in nitrogen, creating a magic compost mix complete with micro-organisms and water.

ACTIVATORS

We usually add 'activators' to our compost to help speed up the process. Perhaps the most basic way of boosting your compost heap is to add some compost from an old compost heap or simply some good topsoil that will contain plenty of micro-organisms to get a new one off to a good start. Other activators include:

- Comfrey leaves – as an activator, comfrey is second to none and a few leaves every so often will help boost your results.
- Grass cuttings – an easily available activator, best added in thin layers regularly to keep the composting process running efficiently.
- Manure – add manure in thin layers and modest quantities. Chicken droppings work extremely well as an activator. Other animal manure is good, too – apart from dog and cat faeces – but let it compost for a bit first before adding it to your heap.
- Nettles – nettles are very common and can be cut for composting twice a year.
- Urine – most people agree that men's urine tends to be a better activator than women's due to hormone levels, so consider putting a 'please pee here' sign next to your compost heap.

some small holes in, leave them for about a year and then enjoy. If you are planning to make leaf mould on a larger scale,

1

SPRING

INTRODUCTION TO

SPRING

Early spring days can be misleading, as winter can hold on or revisit, bringing harsh frosts. When you launch into your spring activities you have to be aware that it will be late spring before growing weather can be guaranteed. The lengthening of the days is like a trigger for plants, and it is the weeds that will tell you growing has begun, as they are optimized to make the most of your garden environment.

PREPARING FOR PLANTING

In early spring, 6 weeks before the date of your local forecast for last frosts, you should start to prepare your vegetable plot. If you need new beds mark them out now, and you can lay newspaper 6 sheets thick, or paper sacking, over the soil, with a thick layer of compost on top. This will prevent weeds growing, then the bed can be dug over in late spring to turn in the compost.

Sterilize all your pots, rinse and then sow seeds under cover ready for transplanting outside when it's warm enough. Build any supports you need for your plants, such as sticks and canes for peas, beans or squashes.

SOWING

Even with very little experience it is possible to take a packet of seeds and grow something in the earth. It is always best to choose your seeds early, so that you are ready to sow at the right time. Preparing the ground is where the hard work has to be done; the actual sowing and planting is a rather delicate task. Seeds sown in rich, moist compost are probably going to germinate and start to grow; however, thinning the seedlings and giving them enough space, depth of soil, the correct

position and enough water is necessary for a bountiful harvest.

SUCCESSION SOWING

It makes sense not to plant all your crops at once, otherwise there will be a period when you will have more ripe produce than you can possibly use. Succession sowing is a simple process: if you wish to harvest crops such as peas, salad, carrots or beetroots throughout the summer and early autumn, start sowing early and sow more every few weeks so that you have plants maturing over a long period of time. You just need to sow enough for each harvest period.

Peas are a great choice for a succession of harvests, as they can be enjoyed at 3 different stages: the young pea shoots, the flat pea pods and finally, the ripe peas in the pods.

ANNUALS & PERENNIALS

Not all plants mature over a single spring and summer, and lots of us hesitate to plant for the longer term. Annual plants have a life cycle that lasts only a year, whereas perennial plants return year after year. Asparagus is the perfect example of a perennial vegetable that takes several years

Now is the time to go outside and start working in your garden

Prepare your pots and containers for the new season

from seed to harvest. The globe artichoke is another example of a plant whose productivity is better in the second year.

CONTAINERS

If you are short of space, there is still time to plant up container-grown produce. Fruit trees and bushes, including slightly more unusual plants such as figs and vines, are well suited to container growing. They will need to be dwarf stock that is pruned to keep them small and fed regularly. We have also successfully grown potatoes, tomatoes, courgettes and squashes in grow-bags or compost-filled baths, buckets or bins.

It might also be worth considering growing crops off the ground on shelves or trellises. We have grown tomatoes, cucumbers, strawberries and beans in hanging baskets.

PLANNING AHEAD

Without planning you can end up with too much produce ready to harvest in the summer months, but with nothing in your garden in the leaner months. The easiest way to avoid this is to set down your plans in a notebook. Write a list of those crops you enjoy in a column on the left-hand side of the page and then create 12 more columns (one for each month of the year through to the following spring), then write a 'P' in the month when you need to plant the crop and an 'H' in each month you will harvest it. This makes it very easy to see at a glance what you will have available to eat in your kitchen garden each month.

For early-season vegetables you need to plant for the year ahead, or indeed the next year; for example, brassicas are among the vegetables that can be harvested in the spring, after the best part of a year in the ground. It is this planning for the future that makes our connection to the garden, and there is something grounding about sowing seeds in spring, then planting the seedlings out, protecting them from caterpillars, tending them and finally harvesting them the following year when there is not much else about in the garden. We never quite know what will happen, of course, so it's best not to count your chickens and make sure you diversify.

SPRING TASKS

- Plan your planting for the season.
- Rotate your crops so your beds are not depleted of nutrients.
- Make sure your soil is dry enough to work before you start digging over beds, as stepping on sodden soil will compress it: a ball of soil formed in your palm should fall apart when you open your hand.
- Start propagating early, as time lost in spring may mean plants don't reach maturity.
- Build a cold frame to help with early propagation.
- Sterilize your pots.
- Sow vegetables inside or under glass, then transplant outside.
- Plant out seedlings when you are sure the frosts have passed.
- Thin seedlings ruthlessly, as plants need space to mature.
- Succession sowing will let you harvest crops all summer and into early autumn.
- Deal with weeds when they are small – hoeing is the quickest way.
- Allow for wildlife corridors in your plot.
- Some insects are allies, so don't exterminate them all with chemicals.
- Apply mulch to your soil to help keep weeds down and moisture in.

METHOD #1

PEAS

Peas are a great crop to grow early under cover. They are also ideal for succession sowing every couple of weeks, in order to have a regular supply over the winter, spring and summer. Peas are best eaten as soon as possible after harvesting, before their sugars start turning to starch. The first peas of the year are delicious raw, straight from the plant. When the peas are still tiny the immature flat pods can even be munched whole, as mangetout.

WHEN TO SOW *autumn to early summer*

SOWING DEPTH *5cm (2 inches)*

DISTANCE APART *seeds 7cm (3 inches), rows 60cm (2 feet)*

WHEN TO TRANSPLANT *when seedlings are 10cm (4 inches) tall*

WHEN TO HARVEST *late spring to early autumn*

SUCCESSION PLANTING *yes*

SOW

Peas like a sunny position and can be grown early under cover or sown outdoors from spring to early summer. Sow the pea seeds in a shallow trench 5cm (2 inches) deep and 15cm (6 inches) wide, in a staggered formation, spaced out 7cm (3 inches) apart. Keep at least 60cm (2 feet) between rows.

An alternative way to sow peas under cover is to use waste lengths of plastic guttering and drill holes in them for drainage. Fill with compost and sow the peas in a staggered formation. When they are big enough and the risk of frost has passed, it is really easy to slide them off the guttering and into a pre-prepared trench.

For a regular supply of peas, sow seeds every couple of weeks from autumn until early summer. Peas take about 12 weeks before they are ready to pick, so make sure you leave enough of a breathing space between sowing.

GROW

If you are growing early peas don't transplant them until any risk of frost has passed. When the peas start to flower, it is important to provide them with extra water for a couple of weeks. This will help the pea pods to swell

Handle gently but firmly ↗

and become delicious and plump. Mulching around the base of the peas will keep the moisture in the surrounding soil. You can use any kind of mulch, but a thin layer of straw is ideal.

Always provide your peas with sticks – this keeps them supported and helps reduce the likelihood of them becoming slug-food. There shouldn't be any need to buy pea sticks, as any twigs and small branches from around the garden will do the job of keeping the peas off the ground and growing upwards. Small branches of fallen hazel work particularly well. Alternatively, use trellis and netting.

COMPANION PLANTING

Sow poached egg plants (*Limnanthes douglasii*) next to your peas. It flowers at the same time and attracts hoverflies and parasitic wasps that will prey on aphids and pests that could damage your crop. The poached egg plant is a perennial, so if you use crop rotation you simply need to dig it up and transplant it each year. Another good reason for planting

it is its flowers, which provide a lovely dash of golden yellow in an otherwise cold and barren month,

PESTS & DISEASES

Pigeons can be a problem. Erect deterrents: a model owl in a nearby tree, old CDs suspended from a stick or netting over the peas when they are young and vulnerable.

HARVEST

Harvest your peas regularly. This will stimulate the plants into producing more flowers and giving you even more peas. You can harvest them when they are very young, at the pod stage, or leave them for longer to become bigger pods. The young pea shoots can be harvested in the spring.

SAVING SEED

If you have a plentiful crop, peas are excellent to dry for seed. Just let the pods dry out a bit while still on the plant, removing them when they start to turn pale, yellow and brittle. Leave the pods on a window sill or in a solar dryer for a week, then take the peas out of the pods and store them in a labelled paper envelope or a glass jar in a dark cupboard until you are ready to sow them.

STORE

Probably the best way to store peas is to freeze them, and the wonderful thing about peas is that they still taste great after being frozen – their sugar doesn't turn to starch so they are deliciously sweet as well as extremely healthy.

EAT

Peas are particularly good boiled briefly and served with butter. Young pea shoots are great eaten raw in salads and also very tasty sautéed in a little butter.

This recipe really shows off the pea's potential. The peas are perfect paired with the mint and goats' cheese, and the pearl barley offers extra bite. It's also a great recipe for using frozen peas if you want to cook it out of season.

SERVES 4-6

50ml (2fl oz) olive oil

400g (13oz) peas

2-4 shallots, finely chopped

100ml (3½ fl oz) white wine

300g (10oz) pearl barley

50g (2oz) chopped fresh mint

500ml (17fl oz) vegetable stock

150g (5oz) soft goats' cheese

salt and freshly ground black pepper

TO SERVE

100ml (3½ fl oz) mint oil

a handful of pea shoots (optional)

12 borage flowers (optional)

PEA & PEARL BARLEY RISOTTO

Heat the olive oil in a large pan, then add the peas and shallots and cook for 3–4 minutes. Pour in the wine and simmer for a further couple of minutes, then add the pearl barley and half the chopped mint. Stir until all the pearl barley is coated with the mixture.

Now start adding the vegetable stock a ladle at a time, waiting until one ladleful is absorbed before adding the next one. Stir evenly and simmer for 20 minutes or so. When all the liquid has been absorbed and the pearl barley has become hydrated, stir in the remaining mint and the goats' cheese and season with salt and pepper.

Serve with a drizzle of mint oil, and garnish with pea shoots and borage flowers if you have any.

METHOD #2

ASPARAGUS

Ideally, asparagus should be eaten within hours of cutting, but even the highly efficient supply chains of the supermarkets would have difficulty achieving that. What's the answer? Grow your own. Asparagus has a relatively short season, so it is important to make the most of it while it is available in abundance -- some asparagus-growing regions even have special festivals celebrating their annual crop. The tips are our favourite part, but don't get rid of too much of the stalk because it's delicious too. Even the tough, woody ends are full of flavour and have their uses in the kitchen.

PLANT

Asparagus takes time to establish itself, so patience is essential. It is usually planted as a 'crown', a root system that is best bought at a year old, but you will have to wait another 2 years before you can hope for heavy crops. To grow your own crowns, sow asparagus seeds thinly in rows 30cm (1 foot) apart and 2.5cm (1 inch) deep. When the seedlings are strong enough, thin to 30cm (1 foot) apart. Nurture for a year, then plant out in mid spring.

GROW

Plant in sunny, free-draining soil. Dig a trench 30cm (1 foot) wide and 20cm (8 inches) deep, sift a 5cm (2 inch) layer of soil over the bottom and spread the roots of the crowns over it, allowing 30cm (1 foot) between the crowns. Finally, cover the crowns with 5cm (2 inch) of soil. Keep 1m (about 3 feet) separation between the trenches. As the shoots grow, keep the trench weed-free and sift over 5cm (2 inches) of soil at a time to cover the shoots. By autumn the trench should be filled.

Don't be tempted to cut any shoots that grow in the first year. Keep weeding around the asparagus and allow the ferny foliage to grow and draw goodness into the root system. You will have to wait until the second year before you get your first harvest.

In the autumn, when the ferns turn yellow, cut them off about 5cm (2 inches) above

WHEN TO SOW *early spring*

SOWING DEPTH *2.5cm (1 inch)*

DISTANCE APART *rows 30cm (1 foot), thin seedlings to 30cm (1 foot)*

WHEN TO TRANSPLANT *the following spring*

WHEN TO HARVEST *mid spring to early summer*

SUCCESSION PLANTING *no*

ground level. In spring, before the spears appear, make a ridge of soil over the rows and apply manure/fertilizer on the top.

PESTS & DISEASES

Slugs like asparagus, too, so be prepared to pop out in the evening with a torch and remove them.

HARVEST

In the second year, you can harvest your crop. When the asparagus spears reach about 10cm (4 inches) above the earth they can be cut about 7cm (3 inches) below the surface. You can buy a special asparagus knife for the task, but any serrated kitchen knife will do. Don't allow the spears to grow too tall, otherwise they become tough. Stop cutting the spears in early summer and allow the plants the rest of the summer to muster their reserves for the next season. If you find your spears are very thin, you have probably cut too many the year before. With a bit of care and restraint, your plants will be productive for up to 20 years, and each crown can be expected to produce up to 25 spears each year.

STORE

Don't even think about storing asparagus — eat it in season and straight from the ground. If necessary, it can be blanched and frozen, or kept in the fridge for a couple of days.

EAT

To prepare asparagus, bend the thick end over until it snaps — this is the point between the tenderest eating part and the tough stems, which are great used in soups. Steam the spears or cook them briefly. We particularly like asparagus chargrilled on the barbecue or a griddle, served with hollandaise sauce.

These are ready to eat

Asparagus has a distinctive flavour that can be removed by overcooking, so it is usually best to steam or blanch it in boiling water for no longer than a couple of minutes. However, in this recipe we do something a little different, sealing the fresh taste of asparagus inside a light batter.

SERVES 4

24 asparagus stalks

vegetable oil, for deep-frying

85g (3½ oz) plain flour

1 tablespoon cornflour

½ teaspoon salt

200ml (7fl oz) sparkling water

4 ice cubes

500g (1lb) lemon sole fillets

FOR THE MAYONNAISE

2 egg yolks

2 tablespoons olive oil

zest of 1 lemon

salt and freshly ground black pepper

TO SERVE

lemon wedges

green salad

TEMPURA ASPARAGUS WITH LEMON SOLE & MAYONNAISE

Snap off the tough end of each asparagus stalk.

Heat some vegetable oil to 180°C (350°F) in a deep-fryer or a large pan. To make the tempura batter, sift the flour into a large bowl and add the cornflour and salt, then whisk in the sparkling water and ice cubes. Don't over-beat the mixture, and use it immediately. Dip the asparagus into the batter and deep-fry them in the oil for 2–3 minutes, or until they are the colour of light golden sand. Fry them in small batches so that the oil stays nice and hot. Drain on kitchen paper and keep warm.

Meanwhile, make a simple mayonnaise by blending the egg yolks either in a blender or by hand, using a fork, and then gently drizzling in the olive oil. When it is fully incorporated, stir in the lemon zest and season with salt and pepper. Set the mayonnaise aside until you need it.

Heat a little oil in a frying pan, then season the fillets and put them into the pan skin side down. Resist the temptation to move them for 2–3 minutes, so that the skin stays intact, then turn them over to cook the other side.

Serve the asparagus with the fish and the mayonnaise, with fresh salad leaves and a wedge of lemon.

CAULIFLOWER

Cauliflowers are large plants that take up quite a lot of space in a vegetable garden. Nevertheless, they are well worth the time and effort involved in growing them: when you succeed in cultivating a huge crown of ornate cauliflower curds, you will experience a serious amount of pride in the garden as well as smiles in the kitchen. We love cooking with cauliflower but we also often eat it raw in salads or dipped into a fondue to enjoy its simple and distinct qualities.

SOW

Different varieties of cauliflower need sowing at different times. If you are growing varieties that will be ready to harvest early in the season, sow under glass or in a cold frame from mid winter onwards. You can sow later varieties outside from mid to late spring. Sow cauliflower seeds in a seedbed before thinning out and transplanting or in specialist seed trays, sowing a couple of seeds into each cell of the seed tray. Sow the seeds in rows 30 cm (1 foot) apart, about 1cm (½ inch) deep and with 7.5cm (3 inches) between seeds.

GROW

Prepare your soil so it is rich in organic material before you transplant your cauliflower seedlings into the ground. Ideally you want very fertile, well-rotted manure beneath the roots of the cauliflower. Keep plants at least 60cm (2 feet) apart.

Water them very well when you plant them, and regularly thereafter. If you miss watering them at some stages the result can be stunted growth and much smaller curds. Regular watering in dry spells is essential for a large cauliflower.

If you want large white curds on your cauliflower, position the leaves over the curd to reduce their exposure to the sun. You can do this by putting a tile or slate over the top of the bent-down leaves or by tying the leaves together, but the best method is simply to fold the leaves carefully over each other. Try not to completely cut off air circulation. The

WHEN TO SOW *mid winter to mid autumn*

SOWING DEPTH *1 cm (½ inch)*

DISTANCE APART *seeds 7.5cm (3 inches), rows 30cm (1 foot)*

WHEN TO TRANSPLANT *mid spring to mid summer*

WHEN TO HARVEST *early autumn to early spring*

SUCCESSION PLANTING *yes*

same technique applies to winter varieties that require protection from frost.

PESTS & DISEASES

Caterpillars can really damage your efforts to grow cauliflowers because they have a tendency to eat the leaves, which then stunts the development of the curds. To avoid this it is essential to protect your cauliflowers with netting, which will stop butterflies laying eggs on your crop.

HARVEST

There is a thin line between waiting for the florets to be ready and them being past their best. If you wait too long, the florets will start to separate and eventually deteriorate. It is best to err on the side of caution and not to be too greedy waiting for them to grow

bigger. When the cauliflower feels firm, use a sharp knife and chop off the head. Keep a few outer leaves on the cauliflower to protect the fragile curds from bruising.

STORE

Soak in salted water for 30 minutes to remove any insects or cabbage worms. Keep whole cauliflower in the fridge for up to 2 weeks, or you can blanch and freeze it.

EAT

The green leaves of the cauliflower are also edible – the small, light green ones close to the white crown are tender, and will add colour to your dish. Or you can try roasting the florets, seasoned and tossed in olive oil, in a hot oven, for about 20 minutes, until golden and tender.

They don't grow this big unless you protect them

Cauliflower cheese is one of those comfort foods that just about everyone loves. We prefer our cauliflower crisp and a cheese sauce with a kick. You can use any cheese you like: Gruyère is a great cheese for cooking, but we particularly love making this dish with a mature Cheddar.

SERVES 4

1 large cauliflower

salt

75g (3oz) butter

3 tablespoons plain flour

500ml (17fl oz) milk

1 teaspoon Dijon mustard

2 teaspoons Worcestershire sauce

100g (3½ oz) cheese, grated

CAULIFLOWER CHEESE

Preheat the oven to 180°C (350°F), Gas Mark 4.

Remove the outer layers of the cauliflower, retaining the green leaves nearest the head. Now break it into florets, or use a paring knife to cut the stalk level with the base if you prefer to cook the cauliflower whole.

Bring a large pan of salted water to the boil. Add the cauliflower and simmer for 4–6 minutes. The stalks should still be firm.

Meanwhile, make the sauce. Melt the butter in a pan, then stir in the flour and cook for 2 minutes. Remove the pan from the heat and gradually add the milk, stirring continuously. Once it is all incorporated, return the pan to the heat and bring to the boil, stirring regularly. When the sauce is hot, stir in the mustard, Worcestershire sauce and all but 2 tablespoons of the cheese.

Place the cauliflower in an ovenproof dish and pour over the sauce. Sprinkle the reserved cheese over the top and place in the oven until the top is golden brown – about 20 minutes.

METHOD #4

PURPLE SPROUTING BROCCOLI

There is more to broccoli than the massive solid green heads that can a rival cauliflower for size. Our favourite is purple sprouting broccoli, which crops early in the year. The season is long and you will have the opportunity to enjoy your vegetables for a couple of months.

SOW

Broccoli is a member of the brassica family and needs soil that is rich in organic matter. In the spring, prepare the ground by digging it over and rake if necessary. Then all you need to do is mark out a small line and spread the tiny seeds very thinly. Sow in rows 15cm (6 inches) apart and 1cm (½ inch) deep. When the seedlings grow, thin them out so they are at least 7cm (3 inches) apart. They

will be ready to transplant when they are 7cm (3 inches) high.

GROW

To transplant them to their permanent positions, ease the seedlings out of their seedbed by putting a trowel into the earth beside them, taking care to keep as much soil as possible on the roots. Put the seedlings into holes that are deep enough to allow them to sit about 2cm (¾ inch) deeper than they were growing in the seedbed, then press the soil around the stem and water well. Allow 45cm (18 inches) between each seedling.

Sprouting broccoli needs a little care and attention through the summer. Keep the weeds down in the rows – hoeing is the easiest way to do this, as the broccoli plants are large and well spread out.

PESTS & DISEASES

Caterpillars can be a bit of an issue, but as long as the plants are not devastated they should recover over the latter part of the year, prior to harvesting the following spring. We prefer to avoid caterpillars rather than to wage war on them: cover the plants with nets as they grow to keep the butterflies away.

HARVEST

Harvest when the flower shoots are well formed but before they open. If you leave harvesting too long and the flowers start to open, the stalks will be tough and woody. When you harvest, cut the central spears first – the rest will continue to grow, and in subsequent harvests you should work your way down the plant. As long as you continue to harvest, you should get nearly 2 months of cropping. Keep cutting even if you don't need to eat the broccoli, or the plant will stop producing florets.

STORE

Store in the fridge for up to 4 days and use before it wilts. Blanch broccoli before you freeze it.

EAT

The best way to cook broccoli is to steam it gently for 4–5 minutes, until al dente. But it's great raw, too.

WHEN TO SOW *early to late spring*

SOWING DEPTH *1cm (½ inch)*

DISTANCE APART *rows 15cm (6 inches), thin seedlings to 7cm (3 inches)*

WHEN TO TRANSPLANT *late spring to early summer*

WHEN TO HARVEST *mid autumn to early spring*

SUCCESSION PLANTING *no*

Colourful, healthy and very tasty

Broccoli requires very little cooking, as it's lovely even when eaten raw. This stir-fry is healthy, crisp and flavoursome. You can serve it with noodles or rice as a vegetarian meal, or it can make a substantial vegetable accompaniment.

SERVES 4

1kg (2lb) tenderstem or purple sprouting broccoli

1 red pepper

½ an onion

1 pak choi

1 carrot

3 tablespoons soy sauce

3 tablespoons orange juice

2 teaspoons cornflour

1 tablespoon honey

4 tablespoons sesame oil

1 garlic clove, crushed

1 teaspoon finely chopped fresh ginger

BROCCOLI STIR-FRY

Separate the broccoli florets if the heads are large and discard any tough stems. Slice the other vegetables. Mix the soy sauce, orange juice, cornflour and honey in a small bowl and set aside.

Heat a wok until very hot, then add the sesame oil. Once the oil is hot, add the sliced vegetables and broccoli. Toss once, then add the garlic and ginger and keep tossing and cooking for about 3 minutes more.

Pour in the soy sauce mixture and stir well. Cook for a couple of minutes, then serve.

2

SUMMER

INTRODUCTION TO

SUMMER

This is the time of year when you really get to enjoy the rewards of the hard graft you put in over the spring. There is always a huge amount of produce ready to harvest, and the weather tends to be well suited to eating outside and enjoying the longer evenings. That said, there is still work to be done and crops to be maintained.

MULCHING

A mulch is a material laid on the surface of the soil (we use old cardboard and straw) that kills weeds by denying them sunlight, while also conserving precious water and protecting the soil from erosion. It is a technique that we use all round the vegetable garden in summer, and it really helps make time to enjoy the weather rather than becoming a slave to it.

WATERING

Watering is one of those summer jobs that requires constant attention, but we try to employ a 'no-watering' policy with most of the crops we grow outside. The basic premise of this approach is that once a seedling has been transplanted and thoroughly watered in, it is then left to grow without being watered. At first the plant will look a little unhealthy and will struggle, but this is only while the roots go down deeper to find the natural water table. Then, having developed a strong taproot, the plant thrives over the drier periods due to its resilient root formation. It's a great way to save water in the garden and cuts down on a lot of the effort of watering. We have found great success using this method, with courgettes and squashes in particular – a perfect technique for hot and slightly lazy summers.

However, the more fragile and exotic plants in the greenhouse require more moisture, so it is a good idea to use an irrigation system set up to water them automatically. All you need is a 12V battery, a demand pump and a timer, plus a collection of irrigation pipes from your local garden centre – a variety of droppers, misters and some leaky hose. This system can be adapted to fit into your water butt or any other water supply, and the time saved is well worth the effort of installing it.

SAVING SEED

We try to save as much seed as possible in order to save money and make the most of all our vegetables. In the garden, among the easiest seeds for the novice seed-saver are peas and beans. The key to success with these is to leave the seed pods to dry naturally on the plant for as long as possible until the pods are papery and bone-dry. Once they have been 'de-podded', leave the seeds to dry in a warm, airy place until they are completely dry, then pack them away in paper envelopes, jam jars or anything else that can be properly sealed and labelled. Whatever you do, don't keep them in your shed or greenhouse – the extremes of temperature can be devastating. An indoor cupboard or drawer is ideal. For the best results, sowing sooner rather than later is

Not every juicy little tomato will make it all the way back to the kitchen ...

preferable, but as with much gardening, trial and error is the name of the game!

TO DIG OR NOT TO DIG

The normal reasons for digging in the garden are to incorporate manure and compost, remove or bury weeds and create soil with a good physical condition, or tilth, for sowing. However, there is an alternative approach to growing that maintains that there is little or no reason to dig. In no-dig gardening the soil is never turned over, and all manure, compost and other organic material is applied to the surface 2 or 3 months before sowing and left to disappear over time. No-dig follows the philosophy of feeding the soil, not the plant. This approach is also extremely useful in summer, when the ground is dry and rock hard.

The no-dig approach focuses on avoiding the disruption of the soil and its worms and their allies, which will actually do the digging for you. Earthworms are working on a permanent and ongoing basis that is arguably far better than a spade or a fork! Additionally, almost 80% of the soil's microbes live in the top 5cm (2 inches) of earth, and these microbes are the key to a soil's fertility. By digging and constantly putting them back below the surface you can damage the soil's ability to generate its own richness.

Digging is definitely a quick and satisfying way of clearing ground that is covered in annual weeds, but sadly the benefits can be short-lived. Some weeds may be killed by burying them, but in the process other dormant weeds will be turned up to the

sprinkling aubergines with salt will draw out moisture

surface and start to germinate, which creates as many weed problems as it solves. Basically, it's more efficient to get rid of the weeds by shallow hoeing or mulching before they become a problem, or by putting down a decent layer of light-excluding mulch for at least a growing season. Nevertheless, even ardent no-diggers would agree that digging to incorporate organic matter into a new garden can still be worthwhile, especially if there's raw clay or silt soil.

HANGING BASKETS

Why not make the most out of aerial space by mounting a bracket on a wall or hanging edible hampers from existing trellis? Making hanging baskets is a great way to creatively reuse materials and salvaged scrap. We have made them out of old shopping baskets and plant pots hung with wire, and woven our own with coppiced willow offcuts.

The advantages of hanging baskets are that they are a mission impossible for pests like slugs and snails (especially if you use copper wire to hang them) and they fill otherwise vacant space. Unfortunately, they tend to dry out quickly so keep your eye on them and water regularly.

WEEDING

Your vegetables are not the only things that will be thriving with the longer daylight and sunshine hours. Weeds will be crowding your edible beauties and competing with them for nutrients and light. Here are a few weeds to look out for:
- Dandelions – These grow in between cracks in pavements, in freshly dug vegetable beds and even in lawns. We find that the best tools for removing them are a small fork or a more specialized narrow

fork that enables you to dig out the root deep down.
- Bindweed – This is a plant that seems to do nothing useful. Bindweed is a curse in the garden because it can strangle other crops. The only answer is to keep digging it up, let it dry out and then burn it.
- Nettles – The best way to clear nettles is by hand, wearing gloves to pull up the roots. Pulled nettles are extremely useful as a compost heap activator (see page 21).
- Grass – In order to stop grass spreading in your vegetable patch, use a mulch (see page 46). Another effective way to build a barrier to grass is to have a decent sharp edge or drop into your vegetable beds – this trench makes it harder for the grass roots to spread while also making weeding easier at the same time.

SUMMER TASKS

- Check container plants and water them regularly.
- Open the vents in the greenhouse or leave the door to your polytunnel open during the day.
- Keep harvesting cut-and-come-again salads.
- Succession sowing will ensure you continue to have crops to harvest later in the year.
- Thin out root crops if sown too close together.
- Pinch out the growing tips of climbers such as cucumbers, grapevines and melons.
- Support climbing beans and peas with trellis.
- Mulch around squashes, courgettes and pumpkins.
- Be careful when watering tomatoes – the fruit will split if the plants are overwatered.
- Use netting to protect brassicas from pests.
- Dry your onion crop while the weather is still good.

METHOD #5

SWEETCORN

It wasn't long ago that we started growing our own sweetcorn and we didn't succeed straight away, but eventually we learnt how to get good results and a proper home-grown crop. There are lot of varieties available, so do a little research and choose the one that will best suit your garden. Sweetcorn is categorized by its sweetness, the time of year it will mature (early, mid season or late) and its colour (it can be white, yellow, or a mixture of the two).

WHEN TO SOW *mid to late spring*

SOWING DEPTH *2.5cm (1 inch)*

WHEN TO TRANSPLANT *when 10–15cm (4–6 inches) tall*

DISTANCE APART *45cm (18 inches)*

WHEN TO HARVEST *mid summer to early autumn*

SUCCESSION PLANTING *no*

SOW

In mid to late spring, sow kernels into small pots or module trays at a depth of 2.5cm (1 inch). If you are using a larger pot, sow a couple of seeds in each pot and thin the seedlings out later when one has established itself as stronger.

GROW

Protect the seedlings from frost and harden the seedlings off gradually. Transplant them when they are 10–15cm (4–6 inches) tall. Sweetcorn is wind-pollinated and needs to be planted in blocks rather than rows. Leave 45cm (18 inches) between plants and position them in a cross formation. Sweetcorn needs a sunny position, sheltered from strong winds. If your garden is very windy, use stakes to support the plants. When the sweetcorn is in flower make sure to give it extra watering.

To improve your chances of getting full cobs of sweetcorn with plenty of ripe kernels

Twist off the ripe cobs ↗

discourage them. Cut a ring of plastic from a 2 litre (3½ pint) bottle and chop a sharp zigzag shape around the top. We've found that this effectively protects the vulnerable stems. You could also try putting coffee granules, sheep-wool, slug pellets or copper tape around the base of the plants.

HARVEST

Harvest your sweetcorn when the tassels have started to turn brown and the kernels are a golden colour. Not every variety will be bright yellow, so a good test is to squeeze a kernel and if it gives out a little cream-coloured substance then they are ready to harvest. If what comes out is clear and watery, leave the sweetcorn for a little longer. When you pick your corn, twist the whole cob off the plant.

inside, tap the tassels that sprout out of the top of the cobs. This will help the plants to pollinate successfully.

COMPANION PLANTING

There is a classic inter-planting technique that works incredibly well with sweetcorn. Plant courgettes, squash or pumpkin around the base of the plants. These help to retain the moisture in the soil, due to their big leaves, and also reduce weed growth by keeping the soil shady. Then plant some climbing beans around the foot of the sweetcorn so that they can grow up it. The stem of the sweetcorn will serve as a natural trellis for the beans to grow up. The advantage to this style of growing is that you end up with 3 crops all being productive in the same space – excellent if you are short of gardening space.

PESTS & DISEASES

Slugs and snails can be a problem. Surround your young transplants with a plastic bottle to

STORE

Sweetcorn is at its very best just after it has been picked, but the flavours and sweetness will fade as soon as the sugars begin turning to starch, so it is best to use it within a couple of days of harvesting. However, you can freeze whole cobs – blanch them for about 5 minutes and then freeze them in a sealed freezer bag. Alternatively, you can spread the kernels on a baking sheet and dry them in an oven set at a very low temperature for 10–12 hours. Rehydrate the dried kernels for 6 hours before using them.

EAT

We particularly enjoy eating corn on the cob – sweetcorn is delicious boiled and smothered in melted butter with a little seasoning. You could also try marinating cobs and cooking them on the barbecue, or roasting them in a hot oven (with the husks still on) for 8–15 minutes.

We particularly like these colourful sweetcorn fritters, as they are quick to cook and absolutely delicious. As the kernels you slice off the cob will not be uniform in size, the larger ones will be 'al dente' while the smaller ones will soften, making for a fritter with a lovely texture.

SERVES 4

2 whole sweetcorn cobs (approximately 250g/8oz sweetcorn kernels)

2 garlic cloves, finely chopped

1 teaspoon paprika

2 limes

4 spring onions, sliced

2 tablespoons chopped fresh coriander

1 egg, beaten

salt and freshly ground black pepper

4 tablespoons plain flour

3 tomatoes

½ a red onion, finely diced

1 fresh red chilli, finely chopped

4 tablespoons mayonnaise

vegetable oil, for frying

green salad, to serve

SWEETCORN FRITTERS WITH SALSA & LIME MAYO

Slice the sweetcorn kernels off the cob and place them in a bowl with 1 of the chopped garlic cloves, the paprika, the zest of 1 lime and spring onions. Then remove half the mixture from the bowl and place in a blender. Blitz on the pulse setting for a minute or two, so that the mixture is fairly smooth, then return it to the bowl and add 1 tablespoon of the chopped coriander and the beaten egg. Stir together, season with salt and pepper and mould into 8 small balls. Dust the balls with flour as you shape them and put them on to a plate in the fridge for 5 minutes while you prepare the salsa and mayo.

To make the salsa, roughly chop the tomatoes and place them in a bowl with the red onion, chilli, the remaining chopped garlic, the juice of 1 lime and the rest of the coriander.

For the lime mayo, put the mayonnaise into a small bowl, squeeze the juice of the second lime into it and stir until incorporated.

Heat a couple of tablespoons of vegetable oil in a frying pan and cook the fritters for 3–5 minutes on each side, pressing them down into flat shapes so that they cook evenly. Drain on kitchen paper to remove any excess oil and serve with the salsa, lime mayo and salad.

COURGETTES

If you have never grown your own vegetables before, courgettes are the ones to start with. They are prolific (from one plant you can expect to get upwards of a dozen fruit) and they are ridiculously easy to grow. There are many different varieties available to grow from seed -- large ones, round ones and even yellow ones. We tend to choose a selection of heirloom varieties each year.

SOW

Sow courgette seeds to a depth of 1cm (½ inch) below the surface of the soil. A good tip is to sow seeds on their side so that there is less risk of putting them in the soil upside down. Either sow courgettes in 7cm (3 inch) pots in mid to late spring or sow them direct outside in late spring to early summer. If you sow them outdoors, cover them with a cloche or cold frame.

WHEN TO SOW *mid spring to early summer*

SOWING DEPTH *1cm (½ inch)*

WHEN TO TRANSPLANT *late spring to early summer*

DISTANCE APART *1m (3 feet)*

WHEN TO HARVEST *mid summer to early autumn*

SUCCESSION PLANTING *no*

GROW

Plant your courgette seedlings out into the ground, leaving almost 1m (about 3 feet) between the plants. This may sound like a lot of space, but the plants will soon expand to fill it. Dig a hole and fill it with well-rotted manure or good compost before setting in your plant. Water really well for the first couple of days, then try out our no-watering technique (see page 46).

Watering courgettes is best done with the help of a funnel or large plastic bottle. Chop off the bottom of the bottle and remove the lid, then place it neck-down in the soil alongside the plant. Then pour water from a watering can or hose into the bottle. This will effectively stop water from getting on to the leaves, which helps avoid mildew.

Mulch around the base of mature courgette plants with straw or cardboard. This will keep the ground weed-free and moist, while also – and this is particularly important – keeping the fruit off the ground as much as possible.

Courgettes grow extremely well in grow-bags, so if your space is limited, you can still grow a bountiful crop.

Mulch your plants

COMPANION PLANTING

Plant other edible flowers among your courgette crops so that there are extra pollinating insects in the area. Try perennial flowers such as calendula or French marigold and borage. These will provide vivid colour and edible petals that are great to include in summer salads.

PESTS & DISEASES

The only time you need to protect courgettes from slugs is when they are very small seedlings. The coarse leaves of the mature plant help make them resistant to pests. Mulching and careful watering will help reduce the risk of powdery mildew, a common fungal disease in courgettes.

HARVEST

Harvesting courgettes is part of their maintenance. Use a sharp knife to cut your courgette where it joins the stem. Be careful not to hack into any surrounding leaves when you do this. If you pick them regularly when the fruit are 10–15cm (4–6 inches) long and

about as thick as your thumb, you will keep the plant productive for longer. It also means you have delicious young courgettes perfect for cooking. If you lapse in your harvesting duties, don't worry – you will simply end up with marrows, which are just very large courgettes. Marrows can be left to grow until they are enormous.

STORE

Once cut, a courgette will last from 5–7 days before it starts to deteriorate. Ideally, pick them as you want them, and try to use them immediately for the best taste and texture. A large marrow will last slightly longer if kept in a cool, dark storeroom.

EAT

You will in all likelihood end up with a glut of courgettes, but luckily there is more to them than ratatouille: try grating them into salads or risotto, combining them with Moroccan spices or even making a courgette cake. Marrows can be slightly watery but are excellent stuffed or turned into chutney.

Eating flowers is slightly controversial in our house, but every summer we try some new ones. Salads are often spruced up with borage or nasturtiums, and even rosemary and chive flowers make their way on to our plates. Courgette flowers are no exception; and they're delicious stuffed.

SERVES 4

200g (7oz) feta cheese

100g (3½ oz) olive tapenade

2 teaspoons chopped fresh mint

100g (3½ oz) pine nuts

salt and freshly ground black pepper

1 lemon

2 courgettes

2 tablespoons olive oil

1 teaspoon chopped garlic

8-12 courgette flowers

vegetable oil, for deep-frying

85g (3½ oz) plain flour

1 tablespoon cornflour

½ teaspoon salt

200ml (7fl oz) sparkling water

4 ice cubes

STUFFED COURGETTE FLOWERS WITH COURGETTE RIBBONS

First, prepare the filling for the flowers. Cut the feta into small cubes and combine in a bowl with the tapenade, mint and pine nuts. Season with a little pepper and the zest of the lemon.

Slice the courgettes very thinly lengthways, using a potato peeler. Heat the olive oil in a pan and add the chopped garlic. When it sizzles, add the courgette ribbons and stir until evenly coated. Squeeze in the juice of half the lemon and season with salt and pepper. Cook over a low heat for 4–5 minutes, or until the courgettes are soft.

Meanwhile, stuff the flowers. Gently fold back a couple of the outer petals of each courgette flower and make a gap big enough to put the filling inside. Spoon in about 2 teaspoons' worth.

Heat some vegetable oil to 180°C (350°F) in a deep-fryer or a large pan. To make the batter, sift the flour into a large bowl and add the cornflour and salt, then whisk in the sparkling water and ice cubes. Don't over-beat the mixture, and use it immediately. Dip the stuffed flowers into the batter and deep-fry them in the oil for no longer than 2 minutes, or until they are the colour of light golden sand. Drain on kitchen paper to remove any excess oil.

Serve the courgette flowers on a bed of the courgette ribbons.

RADISHES

Many gardeners' earliest memory of a successful horticultural endeavour is a row of bright red radishes. These plants are extremely easy to grow and quick to mature -- the only challenge is picking them at their succulent peak. The best approach is to sow radishes in succession -- you just need to remember to sow the next row before you've eaten the first batch. Radishes come in an impressive number of variants, so be adventurous and try different colours and shapes. Some varieties are even grown for their edible seed pods rather than their roots.

WHEN TO SOW	*late winter to mid autumn*
SOWING DEPTH	*1 cm (½ inch)*
DISTANCE APART	*rows 15cm (6 inches)*
WHEN TO HARVEST	*early spring to early winter*
SUCCESSION PLANTING	*yes*

SOW

One of the great things about radishes is that they can be sown, grown and eaten before some of your slower-growing crops have become big enough to deprive them of light. This means that they can be planted in the gaps between these slower crops and you can make optimum use of the space in your garden. Radishes also have the ability to grow faster than weeds, so if the ground is weeded prior to planting, they will dominate the area.

There are 2 distinct types of radish: the summer and winter varieties. Summer radishes can be sown just about anywhere, but if you are going for the optimum growing conditions, they like a reasonably fertile, well-drained soil. The winter varieties stay in the ground for longer and tend to be larger, so they need to be grown in well-composted soil.

A radish at its best

Sow radishes very thinly, about 1cm (½ inch) deep, in rows about 15cm (6 inches) apart, and cover with a thin layer of soil. Germination will take 4–7 days. When you are sowing, it's worth remembering the size of a radish when you consider how far apart to space your seeds.

GROW

If you have sown the seeds too close together, you will need to thin out the seedlings. You can do this when the first roots form (or even earlier, if your seedlings are particularly overcrowded): simply put a finger and thumb on either side of the seedling and then pull it up with your other hand, with the minimum amount of disturbance to the ground. Radishes thrive when you water them regularly. If you don't water in mid summer you can have disappointing crops.

SAVING SEED

If you have a row of radishes that has gone to seed, pick the seed pods when they have dried and open them up to collect the seeds, which you can use for planting your next crop. Radish seeds can be successfully stored for up to 5 years. Label each batch and keep in an envelope.

PESTS & DISEASES

Protect your young seedlings from slugs and snails – try beer traps (see page 67) or egg-shell barriers. Radishes can also suffer from flea beetle attacks. These small insects will nibble holes in the leaves of your plants, weakening them and reducing productivity. Rather than using pesticides, you could try making a trap by putting some treacle or syrup on a piece of cardboard: hold it up to the plants to encourage the flea beetles to hop on to the sticky part of the trap.

HARVEST

Summer salad radishes can be harvested from the moment they are bulbous. Ideally, they should be about 1.5cm (¾ inch) in diameter, depending on the variety, as they are at their best when young. You can leave them to grow larger, but they can become woody and even hollow. You can either harvest winter radishes in November and store them, or leave them in the ground and dig them up as needed.

STORE

Radishes are meant to be eaten when they are fresh and crunchy, though they can be kept in the salad compartment of the fridge for a couple of days.

EAT

Radishes are well suited to adding to salads – try finely sliced radish, fennel and thin segments of grapefruit, especially with a light dressing, or how about adding to coleslaw?

Crisp, wafer-thin slices of radish look stunning in a salad. This recipe marries the soft, rich flavours of rare beef with crisp salad vegetables. The fillet steak is quite expensive, but a little goes a long way.

SERVES 4

200g (7oz) tail end of fillet steak

salt and freshly ground black pepper

12 radishes

1 stalk of celery

a small handful of rocket or watercress

3 teaspoons horseradish sauce

4 tablespoons crème fraîche

BEEF & RADISH SALAD

Remove the steak from the fridge 30 minutes before you want to cook it to allow it to reach room temperature.

Heat a dry frying pan or griddle pan until very hot. Pat the beef dry with kitchen paper and season with salt and pepper. Sear the meat for about 30 seconds on each side, as well as on the ends, then set aside aside for at least 10 minutes.

When you are ready to serve the salad, finely slice the radishes and celery and break the rocket or watercress into individual leaves. Mix the horseradish and crème fraîche together in a bowl.

Slice the beef and arrange the slices on a serving plate. Scatter the celery, salad leaves and radishes over the beef, then drizzle with the horseradish dressing and serve immediately.

Sear the ends, too

GLOBE ARTICHOKES

Globe artichokes are one of our favourite perennial plants. We all want edible plants that not only taste delicious but also look great, and globe artichokes are the perfect answer. With their long silvery leaves, pale green heads and purple thistle-like flowers, they are among the most striking and architectural veggies around. Globe artichokes are not related to the rather less attractive Jerusalem artichokes, but they grow just as tall, making them ideal as a windbreak to protect the rest of your vegetable plot. They are a little tricky to prepare, but if you follow our simple instructions you can't go wrong, and it'll be well worth the effort.

SOW

Sow seeds in early to mid spring in 7cm (3 inch) pots. Sow 2 seeds to a depth of 1cm (½ inch) and thin out the weaker of the 2 seedlings. An easier, but more expensive, option is to buy a container plant and bring it on in your garden.

GROW

Transplant the seedlings into the ground, leaving at least 1m (about 3 feet) between plants and remembering to water them in well. Weed around the base of the plants as normal, mulch over winter with straw to protect them from the cold and water them in summer if it gets very dry.

If you want to expand your crop, you can divide up the root stock and move it to a new spot to give each young plant more space. There is very little else that you need to know – essentially they are a hardy perennial that is a pleasure to work with.

The advantage to artichokes in general is that they will multiply. Shoots spring up from their root system, so year on year you could have more productive plants. If you don't have the space for more, trim these shoots or divide the plants and share them with a friend.

PESTS & DISEASES

Slugs can be an issue for globe artichokes, especially if the plants are grown in the damp

WHEN TO SOW *early to mid spring*

SOWING DEPTH *1cm (½ inch)*

WHEN TO TRANSPLANT *the following spring*

DISTANCE APART *1m (about 3 feet)*

WHEN TO HARVEST *mid summer to early autumn*

SUCCESSION PLANTING *no*

areas these creatures enjoy, so go on the hunt for them after dark with a torch or set some beer traps (see page 67). The artichoke heads can also be infested by aphids, but in most cases you won't need to spray the plants, as the damage can usually be tolerated.

HARVEST

Every year these plants produce abundant harvests. You want the immature flower buds, as you will be eating the leaves and the heart (the bottom of the flower). From mid summer onwards, cut buds from the stem using shears or secateurs. Depending on the variety, harvest them when they are anything from the size of a tennis ball to that of a small melon. Pick the buds when they feel heavy for their size, but before they flower. Often you will find that you get a second harvest later in the season. Remember that artichokes are a member of the thistle family, so wear gloves and take care when picking them.

STORE

Artichokes will keep for a few days once picked. If you want to store them for longer, peel, prepare, blanch and griddle them before preserving them in olive oil with lemon and herbs. You can also dry the thistle heads and use them as decorative ornaments.

EAT

To prepare artichokes, cut the tough, thorny tops off the outside leaves and rub any cut areas with lemon to avoid discoloration. Then use a sharp, serrated knife to cut off the top 3cm (1¼ inches) or so of the inner leaves. Pull out any small pinkish leaves from the centre and use a teaspoon to scrape out the choke – the fuzzy hairs in the middle. Now snap off the stem, remove any tough outer scales and put the prepared artichoke into a bowl with water and lemon juice until cooking time. Boil them for 30–40 minutes and serve with melted butter or hollandaise.

Artichokes don't need much attention while they are growing, but preparing them for the table requires a little effort. However, the treat at the end of the hard work is a pleasure. This dish plays heavily on the proven pairing of globe artichokes with hollandaise sauce.

SERVES 4

FOR THE ARTICHOKES

4 globe artichokes

1 lemon

2 tablespoons olive oil

1 tablespoon chopped fresh parsley

1 teaspoon capers

1 teaspoon chopped gherkins

FOR THE HOLLANDAISE SAUCE

2 tablespoons white wine vinegar

1 tablespoon water

2 egg yolks

100g (3½ oz) butter, melted

salt and freshly ground black pepper

FOR THE PRAWNS

vegetable oil, for deep-frying

2 eggs, separated

150g (5oz) plain flour

200ml (7fl oz) beer

400g (13oz) king prawns

ARTICHOKES & PRAWNS

Prepare the artichokes following the instructions on page 63 and chop into pieces. Grate the lemon zest and set aside for later.

Bring a large pan of water to the boil and add a sprinkling of lemon juice. Plunge in the artichokes and simmer for 3–4 minutes, then remove from the pan and pat dry. Heat the olive oil in a large frying pan, add the artichokes and cook them for about 6 minutes, turning them frequently, until golden and tender. Stir in the parsley, capers and gherkins, then transfer them to a bowl, set aside and keep warm.

To make the hollandaise sauce, put the vinegar into a small pan with the water. Place the pan on a high heat and reduce until there is only 1 tablespoon of liquid left. Allow to cool, then put into a blender with the egg yolks. Slowly add the melted butter to the blender, mixing until an emulsion is formed. Season with salt and pepper and then pour the sauce over the warm artichokes.

To cook the prawns, first heat your oil for deep-frying to 180°C (350°F). Whisk the egg yolks in a bowl with the flour, salt and black pepper, then add the beer and whisk to a smooth batter. Whisk the egg whites until stiff and fold in. Dip the prawns into the batter and deep-fry them, a few at a time, for 2–3 minutes, then remove them with a slotted spoon and pat dry with kitchen paper. Add the prawns to the bowl of artichokes, scatter the lemon zest over the top and serve.

SALAD LEAVES

Salads are the quintessential summer food – they are thirst-quenching and succulent, tasty and packed with goodness. The added bonus is that given the right environment they can be grown all year round. The other reason to grow your own salad is that you can choose a combination of varieties that you won't find anywhere else.

SOW

You can start to grow salads in late winter if you have an undercover area, such as a greenhouse or a sunny window sill, in which to sow the seed. In early spring you can plant the seedlings outside under a cold frame or cloche. The safest and more frost-free time to grow is from early spring until mid summer, sowing them straight into the ground.

Sow more of the same crop every couple of weeks to ensure a good, constant supply over the entire growing season. If you want to have salad over the winter, sow in late summer and cover with protective cloches in mid autumn. You can also buy some specialist winter varieties to give you the best chance of having a supply of salad leaves all year round.

Sow the seeds thinly in good compost to a depth of 1cm (½ inch) and in rows 30cm (1 foot) apart. You can use a riddle to cover

WHEN TO SOW *year round*

SOWING DEPTH *1cm (½ inch)*

DISTANCE APART *rows 30cm (1 foot), thin seedlings to 15cm (6 inches)*

WHEN TO TRANSPLANT *when seedlings are large enough to handle*

WHEN TO HARVEST *year round*

SUCCESSION PLANTING *yes*

the seed drills with a fine layer of compost so that it is easier for the seedlings to sprout through to the sunshine.

GROW

Thinning salads is vital to growing a successful crop. Ideally you want to have at least 15cm (6 inches) between your plants. Water regularly to stop them going to seed early. It is important to try and weed between rows so that the delicate salads aren't competing for light and nutrients.

PESTS & DISEASES

Salads and leafy plants like lettuce are particularly susceptible to slug and snail attacks, so to prevent losing some or all of your crop it is best to take an integrated pest management approach: we recommend using plenty of beer traps and encouraging natural predators.

To make a beer trap, fill several jam jars with 2.5cm (1 inch) of beer and sink them into the ground next to your salad rows. Slugs and snails will be attracted to the smell of the brew and will fall into the jar rather than eating your greens. Planting your crops near a pond is ideal, because your resident frogs will serve as loyal predators and help keep your salads free from pests. Planting a selection of alliums near rows of salad can also help deter slugs and snails because they will avoid the scent.

HARVEST

Try to harvest salads in the morning, when the sap is rising, as this is the time of day when they will be most full of goodness. Some small types such as 'Little Gem' are best harvested by taking the whole lettuce from the ground. Others thrive from a cut-

Ready to harvest

and-come-again style of harvesting. Cut-and-come-again is as simple as it sounds. Use a pair of garden scissors and cut your salad leaves about 2.5cm (1 inch) from the ground. Systematically work your way up and down the beds so that by the time you return to the first plant you harvested it has had time to grow back, ready for round two. Another advantage to this style of growing/harvesting is that it provides more baby leaf salad, which is particularlyl tender.

STORE

Once harvested, salad leaves are best eaten immediately. If you do want to store them, seal in an airtight plastic bag and keep in the fridge for up to 48 hours.

EAT

If you have too many leaves, try cream of lettuce soup: sweat lettuce, onions and garlic in butter, add nutmeg, stock and milk or cream.

This recipe is all about creating a super-healthy salad that will give your body a vitamin boost that puts the idea of just '5 a day' to shame. There is very little dressing in our salad, but feel free to add more or make it richer by adding whatever else you like.

SERVES 4

3 tablespoons extra virgin olive oil

1 teaspoon sliced fresh red or green chilli

200g (7oz) halloumi cheese, cut into 1cm (½ inch) cubes

zest and juice of 2 limes

4 good portions of salad leaves

sprouted beans

1 small head of broccoli, split into florets

1 stalk of celery, diced

1 carrot, cut into matchsticks

1 spring onion, sliced

2 tablespoons toasted pine nuts

SUPER-HEALTHY HALLOUMI SALAD

Heat the olive oil in a frying pan. Add the chilli, swiftly followed by the halloumi, and cook over a high heat for 1–2 minutes on each side, until golden.

Carefully transfer the cheese to a plate and leave it to cool. When the pan has cooled down, add the lime zest and juice and stir to combine.

Divide the salad leaves between 4 bowls, then add the rest of the ingredients and the halloumi. Share the lime dressing between the bowls and serve.

METHOD #10

SPINACH

We all know spinach is good for you. Look at Popeye – he took no nonsense from Brutus after a tin of it. But why eat tinned spinach when it is possible to grow spinach in your garden all year round? There are a staggering number of varieties of spinach, some of which aren't actually spinach at all! Perpetual spinach is a plant that you sow once and then just keep cutting all year long; the flavour and texture are a little different to true spinach, so it is best to pick the leaves when very young and tender.

WHEN TO SOW *early spring to late summer*

SOWING DEPTH *2.5cm (1 inch)*

DISTANCE APART *rows 30cm (1 foot), thin seedlings to 7cm (3 inches)*

WHEN TO HARVEST *mid spring to early winter*

SUCCESSION PLANTING *yes*

SOW

Like any plant with abundant leaves, spinach thrives on rich, fertile soil. It should be sown thinly, in rows 30cm (1 foot) apart and about 2.5cm (1 inch) deep. Water regularly. For succession sowing you should sow more spinach every 4 weeks from early spring, sowing the winter varieties in late summer.

GROW

When the seedlings are large enough to handle, thin them to about 7cm (3 inches) apart. For your first harvest, pull out alternate young plants. The biggest problem you are likely to encounter when growing spinach is the plant's tendency to bolt, at which time productivity all but stops. It is possible to select varieties that are bolt-resistant, but regular succession planting is the easiest and most reliable solution.

PESTS & DISEASES

Spinach is not plagued by many pests, but it can be affected by downy mildew, so water your plants at the base and make sure there is enough space for air to circulate around them.

Harvest when young

HARVEST

Cut mature spinach about 5cm (2 inches) above ground level and the plant will grow to give you a second crop. The plants will be mature after about 10 weeks, but harvest them earlier if you prefer small, young leaves.

STORE

Use spinach immediately, or store in the fridge for up to 3 days. You can also freeze it if you prepare it beforehand: wash the leaves, shake off the water and put them into a large pan with a knob of melted butter. Cover and cook for 3–4 minutes, shaking the pan regularly. When cool, squeeze out excess moisture and put into freezer bags in portion sizes.

EAT

Young leaves are great in salads. Try cooking spinach in a hot, dry pan so it steams in the water left clinging to the leaves after washing.

HOW TO SOW SPINACH

Prepare the ground well. Plant the spinach in drills: make a shallow trough 2.5cm (1 inch) deep and about 5cm (2 inches) wide.

You will be harvesting the leaves young, so the seeds can be sown in rows about 30cm (1 foot) apart.

Cover the seeds with tilth and gently pat the soil down on the seeds. Water the seeds in and keep the soil damp.

Spinach tastes delicious, is quick to cook and really good for you. This speedy recipe uses shop-bought fresh ravioli, but if you have the time it's easy enough to make your own ravioli - filled with more of your spinach, of course.

SERVES 2 AS A STARTER OR 4 AS
A MAIN COURSE

25g (1oz) butter

1 shallot, finely diced

1 garlic clove, crushed

2 handfuls of clean, dry spinach

100g (3½oz) ricotta cheese

a pinch of grated nutmeg

salt and freshly ground black pepper

1 egg, beaten

150ml (7fl oz) double cream

2 tablespoons lemon juice

500g (1lb) fresh spinach and ricotta ravioli

extra virgin olive oil

RAVIOLI WITH CREAMY SPINACH & RICOTTA SAUCE

Melt the butter in a large pan, then add the shallot and garlic and cook gently until softened, without colouring. Add the spinach, pop a lid on the pan, then shake until the spinach is wilted. Set aside to cool, then stir in the ricotta and nutmeg and season with salt and pepper.

Put the spinach mixture into a blender and whizz to a purée. Add the cream and lemon juice and return it to the pan. Heat gently, then pass through a sieve and set aside.

To cook the ravioli, bring a large pan of salted water to the boil; they will take only 2 minutes to cook. At the same time, put the spinach sauce into a pan over a low heat, and warm a little extra virgin olive oil in a frying pan. When the ravioli are cooked, remove them from the pan with a slotted spoon, shake off any excess water, then pop them into the frying pan, toss briefly and serve with the sauce.

METHOD #11

TOMATOES

Tomatoes are an excellent crop to grow at home and do extremely well inside a polytunnel or greenhouse. Some years we get carried away and grow more tomato plants than one family needs, but we always find a way to eat the fruit, and harvesting them never becomes a chore. Anyone who has grown their own tomatoes will agree with us when we say that nothing you can buy will ever taste quite as good as your own!

SOW

Sow seeds in trays or small pots indoors from late winter to mid spring. Put a couple of seeds into each small pot and then separate the seedlings after a few weeks, when 2 leaves have formed.

GROW

Transplant the seedlings to bigger pots, 23cm (9 inches) across, when you see the first flowers appearing. Water regularly and try to keep the plants warm. If you are intending to plant them outside eventually, harden them off gradually by putting the pots outside during the day and bringing them indoors overnight.

As your tomato plants grow taller you will need to support the stems. If you are growing them in a greenhouse, tie them to the roof of the greenhouse with string. If you're growing them outdoors, tie them to a bamboo cane.

Remove any small side shoots near the base, and when your plant starts to get larger, pinch out the suckers that grow at a diagonal angle upwards from the lateral shoots and the main stem. This means that more energy will then go into the established trusses and you will be able to harvest fully matured fruit rather than small ones. It also means fewer tomatoes, but they will be much more juicy. If you are growing your tomatoes indoors, you may want to restrict its height by also pinching out the growing tip when the plant reaches the top of your covered area.

Tomatoes are thirsty plants. Water them regularly and feed with liquid fertilizer every couple of weeks. If you want to avoid the fruit splitting, avoid erratic watering. Remove dead

Pinch out side shoots ⟶

WHEN TO SOW	*late winter to mid spring*
SOWING DEPTH	*cover in compost*
WHEN TO TRANSPLANT	*mid spring to early summer*
DISTANCE APART	*45cm (18 inches)*
WHEN TO HARVEST	*mid summer to mid autumn*
SUCCESSION PLANTING	*no*

or yellowed leaves and fallen fruits as they occur, and try to keep a good air-flow around the plant.

COMPANION PLANTING

The culinary partnership of basil and tomato in the kitchen also works well in the garden. Not only does it make harvesting ingredients for lunch extremely convenient, but growing basil underneath tomato plants deters aphids, whiteflies and spider mites. As a bonus, it will also attract extra pollinating insects to aid with fruit setting.

PESTS & DISEASES

Blight is a serious fungus-like disease that will rot the fruit and leaves of the plant, and can ruin an outdoor tomato crop. You will have to burn any infected plant material. Blight develops in damp conditions, but we have successfully grown tomatoes upside down in hanging containers, and credit this relatively novel approach with eliminating blight in an area prone to the disease.

Leaf mould is a furry grey mould that can grow on leaves if the tomato plants don't have adequate ventilation. If you notice it, remove affected leaves and try to provide more air circulation around your plants. They may have been planted too close together.

HARVEST

Harvest tomatoes either by plucking individual fruit from the plant as it ripens, or by removing entire vines when they are ready. If you harvest the green tomatoes at the end of the season, you can try to ripen them further by placing them under a cloche or close to a ripe banana. But tomatoes are delicious green, too – and they make a great green tomato chutney.

STORE

Refrigerate tomatoes and they will last for a few days. Store them longer term by bottling them or making relish, sauce or chutney.

EAT

Sprinkling salt on roughly chopped tomatoes and leaving them to stand for a few minutes will enhance their flavour and sweetness.

Ripe home-grown tomatoes make a fantastically tasty and near-instant fresh pasta sauce. Choose the ripest, reddest specimens, chop finely and cook them quickly to release all their flavour.

SERVES 4

salt and freshly ground black pepper

500g (1lb) pappardelle

50ml (2fl oz) olive oil

2 garlic cloves, chopped

1 fresh red chilli, seeded and finely chopped

6 fresh tomatoes, chopped

100ml (3½ fl oz) passata

a large bunch of fresh basil

PAPPARDELLE AL POMODORO

Put a large pan of salted water on to boil and when it is bubbling, add the pasta and cook according to the instructions on the packet.

Meanwhile, pour the olive oil into a pan over a medium heat and add the garlic, chilli and two-thirds of the tomatoes. After 5 minutes, when the tomatoes should be starting to soften, add the passata and half the basil. Cook, stirring, for a further 3–4 minutes, then mix in the remaining tomatoes and leave on the heat until the sauce is just warmed through. Season with salt and pepper.

When the pasta is ready, drain it, reserving a little of the cooking water. Toss the pasta with the sauce, adding a little of the cooking water if necessary to loosen it. Tear the remaining basil, sprinkle it over the pasta and serve.

CUCUMBER

When we grew our first cucumber plant we were flabbergasted by the sheer quantity of fruit that it produced. By the end of the growing season one plant had produced 103! This spectacular result hasn't been replicated since, but it says something about the nature of these prolific climbers. Home-grown cucumbers are full of flavour, and come in a much greater variety of textures and shapes than you would ever see in supermarket produce.

SOW

Sow seeds 1cm (½ inch) deep in pots from early to mid spring. Sow the long, flat seeds on their sides so that you don't risk them being upside down by mistake. You can also sow them directly outdoors, but if you choose this as an option try to heat up the ground a bit first, using a cold frame or cloche, and delay sowing until late spring.

GROW

Neck rot is one of the biggest issues with cucumbers and a small raised mound will help protect the stem from getting too damp. So transplant your seedlings into a mound of earth with a handful of well-rotted manure or compost beneath their roots. As they grow, support your cucumber plants with stakes or carefully tie them to a vertical support.

WHEN TO SOW *early spring to early summer*

SOWING DEPTH *1cm (½ inch)*

WHEN TO TRANSPLANT *when 6 weeks old and no risk of frost*

DISTANCE APART *80cm (2½ feet)*

WHEN TO HARVEST *early summer to early autumn*

SUCCESSION PLANTING *no*

Keep the soil around the base moist and feed the plants every fortnight. The main stem of a cucumber plant can grow very tall and will have lateral shoots that need pinching out at the ends, just beyond a flower. About 60cm (2 feet) is a good length for these shoots.

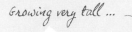

Growing very tall ...

COMPANION PLANTING

One of the biggest pests a cucumber plant faces is the cucumber beetle. A ring of radishes planted around the base of the cucumber will seriously deter the beetle from paying your plants a visit. Dill can also be good planted nearby as it is known to encourage pollinating insects.

PESTS & DISEASES

Having planted your cucumber on a mound to deter neck rot, you can help it even more by placing a cardboard loo roll around its stem as a protective collar. Stick half of this collar into the soil and it will reduce the risk of disease. It will also serve as an indicator of the presence of any cucumber beetles because they will chew holes in it. Put the skins of onions and garlic around the base of the plants to deter cucumber beetles.

HARVEST

Most cucumbers should be harvested when they reach about 20cm (8 inches) in length. Harvest regularly to maintain a prolific crop.

STORE

Keep cucumbers in the fridge and consume within 5–7 days.

EAT

Cucumber is great in a smoked salmon sandwich, but when seasoned well, it's also a surprisingly good filling on its own, in a sandwich made with thinly sliced bread.

When you grow your first cucumber plant you are very likely to be confronted with the challenge of how to eat the many succulent, green vegetables it produces. Cucumbers are refreshing chopped into salads, but our favourite recipe transforms them into a cooling dip.

SERVES 4

1 large cucumber

½ teaspoon table salt

200g (7oz) Greek yoghurt

4 garlic cloves, finely chopped

2 tablespoons chopped fresh mint

400g (13oz) chicken breasts, cut into bite-sized chunks

25-30ml (1fl oz) lemon juice

1 tablespoon olive oil

pitta breads

red onion slices

a handful of mixed salad leaves

TZATZIKI WITH PITTA & GYROS

Grate the cucumber and place in a sieve over a bowl. Sprinkle over the salt and stir. Leave for 5–10 minutes so that some of the moisture can be drawn out – this will avoid a watery dip and keep it tasting fresh.

Put the yoghurt into a bowl and stir in half the garlic and 1 tablespoon of the mint. Add the cucumber, stir and place in the fridge until you need it.

Toss the chopped chunks of chicken breast with the lemon juice and the rest of the garlic and mint. Either heat 1 tablespoon of oil in a frying pan and cook the chicken for 10 minutes until cooked through, or thread the chunks on to kebab sticks and cook them over a barbecue.

Serve the hot chicken with the cool tzatziki, some warm pitta breads, slices of red onion and the salad leaves.

Garlic is good for you!

METHOD #13

ONIONS & SHALLOTS

Over the course of a year, most people use a huge quantity of onions and shallots. The cheapest way to grow your own is to plant seeds and then thin out the plants to give them enough room to flourish, but we have always gone down the easier route of planting onion sets -- immature onion bulbs that grow into big onions. After years of success, it's a system we are very comfortable with; it takes less skill, and the soil need not be frightfully fertile.

WHEN TO PLANT SETS *late autumn (to overwinter) or late winter to mid spring*

PLANTING DEPTH *top of bulb at ground level*

DISTANCE APART *sets 10cm (4 inches), rows 20cm (8 inches)*

WHEN TO HARVEST *mid summer to early autumn*

SUCCESSION PLANTING *no*

PLANT

When growing onions and shallots from sets there is a slightly increased chance that they may bolt and go to seed, so it is always better to go for sets that are no more than 1.5cm (¾ inch) across. Sets are usually sold by weight, so this has the added advantage that you will get more for your money planting this way.

Before you plant them, make sure that the ground is weed-free and rake it over. Plant onion sets about 10cm (4 inches) apart in rows separated by 20cm (8 inches). The sets can be pushed into soft ground, or you can make shallow holes with a dibber and then drop them in so that the top of the bulb is at ground level. It may sound silly, but do make sure you that you put your sets in the ground the right way up!

Each single shallot set will grow into a number of shallots, possibly up to 10. Plant shallot sets in exactly the same way as onions, but further apart because they spread more: at 15cm (6 inches) apart is ideal.

GROW

There are varieties of onion that have been specially developed to be huge, but we would caution against growing for size alone, as the resulting onions can be watery and very mild.

Spring-planted sets will be mature in late summer, so they will be growing throughout the period when your plot will be at its most productive. You will need to keep the weeds down, so regular hoeing is essential. If any bulbs are forced out of the ground by frost or lifted by birds, just push them back into the ground.

PESTS & DISEASES

The onion fly lays its eggs at the base of the onion. Once the maggots have hatched, they eat away at the stems and the bulb. It is not possible to treat onion fly with chemicals, so cover young plants with insect-proof mesh or fleece to keep these pests away.

HARVEST

Leave the onions in the ground for about 2 weeks once the leaves have turned yellow and flopped over in summer. Lift them on a dry day by putting a fork under the roots and easing them out.

Early in the season, when the green shoots of your shallots are about 20cm (8 inches) tall, you can dig up the whole bunch to have what is effectively a bunch of 'spring onions' – great for early salads, or you can leave them to mature and treat as onions.

STORE

Onions and shallots not for immediate use must be dried if you want to store them. Place them on a rack for 7–21 days, preferably in a covered area out of direct sunlight, until the skins are firm and dry. Check them over and keep only the undamaged ones – on trays, in sacks or made into plaits.

EAT

No matter how many onions we grow, we never seem to have enough. The most frequently used and versatile vegetables in our kitchen, they rarely play the starring role: instead, they add depth and flavour to everything from sauces to stews. Caramelized onions are the basis for a classic French onion soup (as well as being delicious on a burger or a hotdog), but you can also bake onions whole, roast them in wedges or turn them into crispy, deep-fried, battered onion rings.

Harvesting onions

Onions are often just a background ingredient, but in a few special dishes, they have a starring role: French onion soup and onion rings are classics. But when it comes to the ultimate partnership of taste and texture, that honour belongs to the onion bhaji. Make a batch to snack on or serve with other spicy Indian treats.

SERVES 4

vegetable oil, for deep-frying

lemons, to serve

FOR THE ONION BHAJI

150g (5oz) plain flour

3 white onions, finely sliced

2 eggs

1 teaspoon coriander seeds, crushed

1 fresh green chilli, finely chopped (optional)

½ teaspoon cumin seeds

½ teaspoon turmeric

½ teaspoon baking powder

a large bunch of fresh coriander leaves, chopped

FOR THE ONION SALSA

1 red onion, finely chopped

1 tomato, seeded and diced

1 tablespoon lime juice

1 teaspoon mango chutney

1 tablespoon fresh coriander leaves, chopped

1 garlic clove, finely chopped

1 tablespoon chopped cucumber

ONION BHAJI WITH ONION SALSA

To make the onion salsa, simply mix all the ingredients together and refrigerate until needed.

To make the bhajis, sift the flour into a large bowl and add the rest of the bhaji ingredients. Gradually add water until the batter starts to thicken and coats all the onion slices. Heat some vegetable oil to 180°C (350°F), in a deep-fryer or a deep-sided frying pan. Carefully spoon dollops of the mixture into the oil and fry the bhajis for 3–4 minutes, or until golden brown. Drain on kitchen paper to remove any excess oil and keep warm.

Serve the warm bhajis with a spoonful of onion salsa and a squeeze of lemon juice.

METHOD #14

GARLIC

Garlic must be one of the most common flavourings in cooking -- it may have originated in central Asia, but it has been embraced by cooks all over the world. Most people have garlic in their kitchen, and what better way to ensure a ready supply than to grow it yourself? If you do decide to give it a go, you will also have the opportunity to use it while it's fresh, or green, and you'll discover that its mild flavour is a real pleasure to cook with. Garlic is really easy to grow, so give it a try.

WHEN TO PLANT *mid autumn to late winter*

SOWING DEPTH *top of clove at ground level*

DISTANCE APART *15cm (6 inches)*

WHEN TO HARVEST *early to mid summer*

SUCCESSION PLANTING *no*

PLANT

There are lots of different types of garlic – some can be as hot as chilli, while others are so mild you could almost eat them like apples. It all comes down to personal choice. There is something very satisfying about growing large, juicy garlic bulbs, not least because there is less peeling required when it comes to cooking.

Buy your seed garlic from a recognized seed merchant to ensure you have a fighting chance of producing the tastiest produce. Some people suggest that any bulb of garlic can be split into cloves and planted; however, there is nothing so frustrating as waiting for 9 months only to have rather disappointing little bulbs.

Plant your garlic in blocks or rows in well-drained soil, which needs to be dug over and weeded in advance. When you split the bulb, take care not to damage the individual cloves. Press each clove into the ground about 15cm (6 inches) apart to have plenty of space for hoeing.

You can overwinter your garlic by planting it from late autumn up to mid winter.

GROW

In dry spells, growing garlic will benefit from a little watering, but apart from that it's just a matter of keeping the weeds down.

PESTS & DISEASES

Like all members of the allium family, garlic can suffer from 'rust', a fungal disease that leads to powdery orange spots on the leaves. Mild attacks won't affect the quality of the bulbs, if caught early enough. But in more serious cases, the only answer is to lift out the crop (don't compost the leaves) and keep the bed free of alliums for at least 3 years.

New season's garlic

HARVEST

During the growing season, you can snip off some of the plants' green leaves to use in salads. When the stalks turn yellow in summer, pull up the mature plants and put them on a rack to dry. Rather than waiting for the garlic to mature, you can harvest it when it is young (known as 'green'). The bulbs just need to be peeled, sliced and used as you would shallots or the mature garlic.

STORE

Garlic bulbs can be plaited or bunched once the stalks have dried out. Store your garlic in a light area with good air circulation, as keeping it in a dark place may encourage it to sprout fresh green shoots. Consume within 6 months.

EAT

With garlic, sometimes less can be more: try rubbing the sides of a salad bowl with a peeled clove before putting your ingredients in. Alternatively, you could try roasting the whole bulbs for 30 minutes at 180°C (350°F), Gas Mark 4. Mash the roasted bulbs with a fork, leave the purée to cool, then use it in sauces and salad dressings.

Imagine pizza crossed with garlic bread - and we don't just mean adding a few slices of garlic, we mean really, really garlicky. This pizza is topped with a purée made from a whole head of garlic, roasted until soft, sweet and aromatic.

SERVES 4

1 whole garlic bulb, plus 2 garlic cloves, finely sliced

extra virgin olive oil

FOR THE PIZZA BASE

1 x 7g sachet of dried yeast

200ml (7fl oz) warm water

½ teaspoon sugar

300g (10oz) plain flour

1 teaspoon salt

GARLIC PIZZAS

Preheat the oven to 200°C (400°F), Gas Mark 6. Place the garlic bulb on a baking sheet and put it into the oven for 30 minutes. Allow the bulb to cool, then scrape out the softened inside of the cloves.

To make the pizza base, mix the yeast, water and sugar in a bowl and set aside for 10 minutes. Sift the flour and salt into a large mixing bowl. Add the yeast mixture and mix well to form a dough. Turn out on to a floured surface and knead for about 5 minutes, then place in a greased bowl and cover loosely with clingfilm. Leave in a warm place for about an hour to rise, then divide the dough into 4 pieces and pull each one into a roughly circular shape with your hands or by rolling out.

Mix a quarter of the garlic purée with a little extra virgin olive oil. Dot several patches of the purée over each pizza base and sprinkle with the garlic slices. Put the pizza on a baking sheet or a pizza tray (or a pizza stone, if you have one), drizzle with extra virgin olive oil and bake in the oven for about 10 minutes, or until golden.

METHOD #15

BROAD BEANS

Broad beans are a hardy vegetable that will survive even a harsh winter. They are a bountiful crop that adds real vibrancy to an often sleepy garden. We always sow a couple of large blocks over the seasons and enjoy them tossed in olive oil in salads, fried with paprika and sea salt, or as a simple side dish with melted butter. The challenge with broad beans is not really growing them but how you play with the ways you cook them.

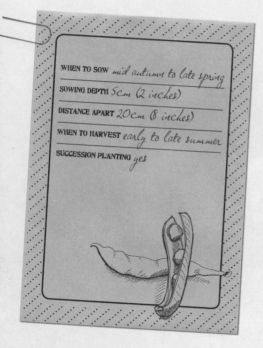

WHEN TO SOW *mid autumn to late spring*

SOWING DEPTH *5cm (2 inches)*

DISTANCE APART *20cm (8 inches)*

WHEN TO HARVEST *early to late summer*

SUCCESSION PLANTING *yes*

To sow, use a dibber or your finger to make a hole 5cm (2 inches) deep and complete a grid of holes with 20cm (8 inches) between each one. Try laying a square piece of wooden trellis on the ground and using it as a grid marker for making the holes. Place a bean in each hole, cover with soil and water in.

If you don't have a large plot, there are dwarf broad bean varieties that are perfect for growing in pots on a patio, and you'll find that because they grow upwards you can get a very decent crop of broad beans for the small space they occupy.

GROW

Once the beans have germinated and are 15–20cm (6–8 inches) tall, raise the wooden trellis, if you've used one, and set it horizontally on 4 simple wooden legs. You want this flat lattice to be about 25–30cm (10–12 inches) above ground level. Secure it with string or wire and wait for the beans to grow through it. Broad beans have a tendency to droop once they start to produce heavy pods, and the danger is that they can lie on the ground and become victim to slug attacks and damp soil. The advantage to this lattice system is that any heavily laden plants are

SOW

Sow broad beans directly into the soil from autumn onwards for an early spring crop, and from early spring if you want to be picking them over the summer. A good spring crop can be ready to pick in as little as 15 weeks, so they provide almost instant satisfaction.

supported by the trellis below them. The result is perfect broad beans. Alternatively, if you're not using trellis, place a stake at each corner of the bed of beans and pass string around the rows so that they have some support.

PESTS & DISEASES

Blackbean aphids can be a real pest and will stunt your crop if they become too established, so remove any leaf tips that have a blackfly problem: pinch out the top few inches of the stem at the time when the pods start forming below. This not only produces a slightly earlier crop but also prevents a pest problem. The bonus is that these delicate tips are also very pleasant to eat. Steam them gently and serve in a warm spring salad or as an accompaniment to fish.

HARVEST

When the beans reach a length of 10cm (4 inches), you can start picking them for cooking, either shelled or as whole pods. Try to harvest them well before they become black or stringy.

STORE

Once picked, store the beans in the fridge and consume within a week. You can also blanch them briefly and then freeze them – it's worth spreading the beans out on a tray first, so that they freeze individually, before putting them into freezer bags or containers. You can try drying podded broad beans and storing them in an airtight container, to rehydrate later. However, this is best done in a professional dehydrator – and unfortunately these don't come cheap.

EAT

You can serve the beans whole in their pods if they are very young, otherwise it's best pod them first. Broad beans are also very good boiled and then passed through a sieve to make a purée. Older broad beans can be tough, but you can peel off the leathery green skin that encases the sweet bit in the middle. This is a time-consuming process, but well worth the effort when you get to the delicious bean lurking inside.

Broad beans grow in vast numbers and that's fine with us, as they are not only delicious but also extremely versatile. This recipe is simplicity itself - the key is keeping the broad beans as the main flavour.

SERVES 4

200g (7oz) broad beans (shelled weight)

2 tablespoons chopped fresh mint

150g (5oz) feta cheese, cubed

olive oil

salt and freshly ground black pepper

herb sprouts, to garnish (optional)

BROAD BEAN & MINT SALAD

Heat a pan of water until boiling and then add the beans. Blanch for 3 or 4 minutes, then drain in a colander. When they are cool enough to handle, peel them by using your thumb and index finger or a fingernail to break the layer of skin at the side of each bean. Now just squeeze the bean until the bright green kernel pops out and into your serving dish.

Put the mint and feta together in a bowl, add the broad beans and a drizzle of olive oil, then season with salt and pepper. Serve garnished with herb sprouts, if you have any.

METHOD #16

BEETROOT

The versatility of this vegetable takes many people by surprise. These roots -- and their leaves -- can be enjoyed in many delicious ways; they don't always have to be pickled in vinegar. Beetroots come in lots of shapes, sizes and colours. The main varieties are classified by shape, specifically globe, cylindrical and long. As well as the usual dark red roots, try experimenting with white, yellow or variegated varieties.

WHEN TO SOW *early spring to mid summer*

SOWING DEPTH *2.5cm (1 inch)*

DISTANCE APART *seeds 10cm (4 inches), rows 30cm (1 foot)*

WHEN TO HARVEST *early summer to early winter*

SUCCESSION PLANTING *yes*

SOW

If you want to grow a prize-winning specimen you'll need deep sandy soil in a sunny area. Sow in rows 30cm (1 foot) apart and 2.5cm (1 inch) deep in early spring and then succession sow every 4 weeks until mid summer. Sow beetroot thinly, to get a row of seedlings, and use the thinnings in salads.

Sow the seeds in pairs about 10cm (4 inches) apart and after germination (which will take a couple of weeks), when the seedlings have grown to about 2.5cm (1 inch) tall, thin out the weaker plants leaving single beetroots to grow on. If you are interested in using the roots as well as the leaves, make sure to leave larger gaps between the seedlings so that the beets have space to form.

GROW

Globe-shaped beetroots are the most common and popular, but the cylindrical types of roots are useful for winter storage. Long varieties of beetroot are rather parsnip-like in shape and

need to be grown in soil free from stones if they are to achieve their perfect form.
If the plants do not receive sufficient water they can become very woody and all but inedible, so water them regularly. Keep the weeds down between the rows.

Leaves are tasty, too

PESTS & DISEASES

Beetroot is susceptible to mineral deficiencies: the leaf veins can turn yellow or grey, or brown blotches can appear on the flesh itself.

HARVEST

Pick beetroots before they get too big and tough – about 4cm (1½ inches) diameter is a good size. Put a fork into the ground near the roots and loosen it before pulling the plant out. If the ground is not sufficiently loosened, the stalks will become bruised or they may even get torn off when you pull at the plant – this can make them unacceptable for storage. Fresh beetroots need to be stored with their stalks intact, so avoid cutting the leaves with a knife or it may lead to bleeding. If you wish to remove the leaves, twist them off 5cm (2 inches) above the root.

STORE

Beetroot can be eaten all year round with a little preparation. Roots that are picked fresh and are clamped (see below) in late autumn will be good until the start of spring. Make a batch of pickled beetroot to enjoy while the next year's crop is growing. Small beetroots can be boiled and skinned for freezing.

EAT

You can use beetroot to make beautiful red soups, such as the classic borscht of Eastern Europe, but it is also wonderful roasted and makes a great mash. You can even turn it into a marinade for beetroot-cured salmon. Cook larger beetroot leaves just like you would chard, and treat the smaller, younger ones like spinach (see page 71).

HOW TO CLAMP BEETROOT

Cut or twist off the leaves to within 2.5cm (1 inch) of the root itself.

Place the beetroot in sand, making sure they don't touch. Press sand down between and over them to a depth of 2.5cm (1 inch).

The colour of beetroot is both its blessing and its curse. It makes the most amazingly coloured soup, but you may need to wear rubber gloves when peeling and preparing it to prevent the pink juices causing too much mess. The root's earthy flavour is delicious when made into a sweet soup.

SERVES 4

1 onion, finely chopped

1 tablespoon sunflower oil

200g (7oz) beetroot, diced

1 tablespoon sugar

1 teaspoon ground cinnamon

1 teaspoon ground mace (or a pinch of nutmeg)

400ml (14fl oz) vegetable stock

salt and freshly ground black pepper

50ml (2fl oz) crème fraîche

BEETROOT & CINNAMON SOUP

Put the onion into a pan with the sunflower oil and cook gently until softened, then stir in the beetroot. Continue to cook over a medium heat for 5 minutes, then add the sugar, cinnamon, mace and stock. Bring to the boil, then turn off the heat and leave to cool down a bit.

Whizz in a blender until smooth, then pour back into the pan, reheat and simmer for a further 5 minutes. Season with salt and pepper.

Serve with a spoonful of crème fraîche in the centre of each serving.

AUBERGINE

Members of the nightshade family and relatives of the tomato and potato, aubergines hail from South-East Asia and are actually classed as berries. They require a sunny, sheltered spot to grow and are an ideal crop to grow under glass -- which will all but guarantee a successful crop. Don't expect your crop to look exactly like the fruit you see in supermarkets; ours have tended to be smaller and there is a lot more variation in the colours, but they taste great.

SOW

Sow aubergine seeds in warm, frost-free conditions, in compost-filled pots, in late winter/early spring.

GROW

About 3 weeks after germination the seedlings should be big enough to transplant into larger pots, grow-bags or raised beds. Allow 60cm (2 feet) between plants in a greenhouse, or plant 2 in a grow-bag. At 8 weeks the seedlings should be large enough to transplanted out. When the plant has reached a height of 45cm (18 inches), pinch out the growing tip and stake the plant. To ensure fruit of a reasonable size, limit the flowers to no more than 5 or 6 per plant and water the plants consistently; you can feed them with tomato feed to increase crop size.

PESTS & DISEASES

Glasshouse red spider mite and whitefly can present problems for aubergines, so mist plants regularly to avoid the hot, dry conditions these pests prefer, using sprays based on soft soap or plant oil. Keep an eye out for aphids.

Diseases such as blossom end rot, wilt diseases and various types of blight can be prevented or eliminated by practising crop rotation, weeding and ensuring uniform watering.

HARVEST

From mid summer to mid autumn you can expect to have aubergines to harvest. Cut each fruit when it reaches a satisfactory size –

WHEN TO SOW *late winter to early spring*

SOWING DEPTH *1cm (½inch)*

WHEN TO TRANSPLANT *when 8 weeks old*

DISTANCE APART *60cm (2 feet)*

WHEN TO HARVEST *mid summer to mid autumn*

SUCCESSION PLANTING *no*

We often bake aubergine as the forerunner to making baba ghanoush. By popping the garlic in the oven with the aubergine, the softened flesh of both the garlic and aubergine can be mixed with lemon juice, tahini, olive oil, salt and pepper to make this delicious dip.

Aubergine Parmigiana is a classic layering of fried slices of aubergine, a tomato sauce (with onion, garlic, red wine vinegar and oregano) and grated Parmesan cheese. To make it, repeat these 3 layers twice, finishing with a layer of cheese, and bake in an oven preheated to 180°C (350°F), Gas Mark 4, for 30 minutes.

Aubergines should always be cooked, as the raw fruit contains solanine, which can cause stomach upsets and nausea.

anything upwards of 15cm (6 inches) long, and before it loses its sheen. If the fruits are left too long, as indicated by the loss of shine, they become bitter.

STORE
Aubergines can be kept in a plastic bag in the fridge for up to 2 weeks, provided they have not been damaged.

EAT
Aubergines are delicious sautéed, grilled, baked or roasted. The flesh of the aubergine, which is spongy and slightly bitter when raw, becomes soft and develops a slightly smoky flavour. Some people sprinkle slices of aubergine with salt, leave them for 30 minutes and then pat them dry with kitchen paper before using them, as this is believed to improve the fruit's texture and reduce any bitterness. If we have time, we do this too, as it does reduce the amount of oil the aubergines will absorb.

sadly, you will sometimes have problems

We recommend cooking aubergines quickly and at a high temperature, to bring out their naturally smoky flavour. This recipe uses griddled aubergines and plenty of spices to complement the herby marinade.

SERVES 4

2 large aubergines
table salt
olive oil
salt and freshly ground black pepper
a large bunch of fresh lemon thyme leaves, chopped
couscous, to serve

FOR THE TAGINE
½ teaspoon paprika
½ teaspoon coriander seeds
¼ teaspoon turmeric
½ teaspoon harissa paste
3 garlic cloves
1 fresh red chilli, chopped
1 teaspoon chopped fresh ginger
2 tablespoons vegetable oil
4 chicken legs and 4 chicken wings
1 x 400g tin chopped tomatoes
1 x 400g tin chickpeas
2 lemons, sliced
15 cherry tomatoes

GRIDDLED AUBERGINES WITH CHICKEN & CHICKPEA TAGINE

Cut the aubergines lengthways into slices about 5mm (¼ inch) thick. Sprinkle with table salt and leave on a rack set above a draining board for 5–10 minutes. Next, heat a ridged griddle pan until it is very hot. Lightly brush the aubergine slices with olive oil, sprinkle with salt, pepper and lots of chopped lemon thyme, then place them on the griddle pan for a few minutes each side.

To make the tagine, preheat the oven to 180°C (350°F), Gas Mark 4. Put all the spices, plus the harissa, garlic, chilli and ginger, into a pestle and mortar and grind until they form a smooth, aromatic paste. Heat the vegetable oil in a large casserole and add the spice mix. Stir for about 3–4 minutes, then add the chicken pieces and keep turning until the skin starts to colour evenly. After 5 minutes add the tomatoes, chickpeas, lemons, cherry tomatoes and finally the griddled aubergines. Put into the oven and cook for 45 minutes, until the chicken is tender.

Serve the tagine with a bowl of couscous, mixed with more lemon thyme.

Griddle the aubergines

METHOD #18

POTATOES

Nothing quite beats the taste of potatoes straight from the garden, the skins rubbed off, boiled and served with butter. Potatoes can be classified as earlies, second earlies and main crop. As their name suggests, earlies are ready to harvest much sooner than the others. There are many varieties of potatoes available, with different textures and colours – from reds and white to purple, orange and even black. Try out a few and see how you get on, but make a note of what you have planted where so that you know what you are eating.

WHEN TO CHIT *late winter*

WHEN TO PLANT *earlies = early spring second earlies = mid spring main crop = mid spring*

PLANTING DEPTH *15cm (6 inches)*

PLANTING DISTANCE *tubers 35cm (14 inches), rows 90cm (3 feet)*

WHEN TO HARVEST *earlies = early to mid summer second earlies = mid to late summer main crop = early to mid autumn*

SUCCESSION PLANTING *yes*

CHIT

Potatoes bought from a supermarket may have been treated to inhibit sprouting, so buy seed potatoes. In late winter, lay the seed potatoes in egg boxes or wooden 'chitting' trays – make sure the end with the most eyes is facing upwards – and leave them in a light, frost-free location for 6 weeks to sprout.

When the sprouts are bout 5cm (2 inches) long, the potatoes are ready to plant.

PLANT

Potatoes will grow in almost any type of soil, but if you're planting direct into the ground you'll need to rotate your crop every 2 years to reduce the risk of disease and avoid soil depletion. It is best to prepare the trenches and ground in the autumn. Plant your seed potatoes out in spring, once the earth has warmed up a little. Plant them 35cm (14 inches) apart and about 15cm (6 inches) deep in well-manured trenches. Rows should be about 90cm (3 feet) apart. You can also grow potatoes successfully in sacks and containers.

GROW

If there is a chance of frost, cover any early green shoots that appear with loose soil. If it is really dry you should water the plants,

especially when the tubers are starting to form. When the green leaves (known as the 'haulm') are about 20cm (8 inches) high, it is time for earthing up. Use the soil between the rows and pile it against the side of the shoots, leaving about 5cm (2 inches) of green poking through. Continue to earth up the potatoes as they grow, drawing up the soil over each row to form a ridge.

PESTS & DISEASES

The best defences against the many viral, bacterial, fungal or parasitic diseases that can affect potatoes are sensible crop rotation and planting resilient local varieties.

HARVEST

If you planted your potatoes in early spring, wait until the flowers are open and then check the state of the tubers by gently removing the soil around the roots. If they are big enough,

put the tines of a fork into the ground leaning away from the plant, then grasp the haulm and lift as you ease the soil up. If you planted them later for a main crop you can leave the plants until the stems have completely withered. Take your time when harvesting and ensure you gather even the smallest tubers, otherwise next year you will have lots of unexpected potato plants.

STORE

Once you have harvested the potatoes, leave them to dry for several hours and then store them in a wooden box in a frost-free shed or cold store room, or in a clamp (see age 121).

EAT

Everyone has their favourite way of serving potatoes: roasted, boiled, baked, mashed, bashed, chipped, sautéed, as fondant potatoes or a gratin dauphinois, to name but a few.

Sausages and mashed potatoes were made for each other. Our buttery mustard mash doesn't need any gravy, so we've created a delicious onion marmalade to accompany the dish.

SERVES 4

12 traditional sausages
750g (1½ lb) potatoes
75g (3oz) butter
100ml (3½ fl oz) cream
1 tablespoon wholegrain mustard

FOR THE ONION MARMALADE
1 tablespoon vegetable oil
3 red onions, finely sliced
1 teaspoon mustard seeds
75g (3oz) muscovado sugar
100ml (3½ fl oz) red wine vinegar
100ml (3½ fl oz) water

BANGERS, MUSTARD MASH & ONION MARMALADE

To make the onion marmalade, heat the vegetable oil in a pan. Add the onions and mustard seeds and cook over a low heat until the onions are soft. Add the sugar, vinegar and water to the pan, then bring to the boil and simmer until the liquor evaporates, leaving a syrupy condiment. Set aside while you cook the sausage and mash.

Preheat the oven to 180°C (350°F), Gas Mark 4. Put the sausages into a roasting tin and bake them in the oven for 30 minutes, or until cooked through.

Meanwhile, cook the potatoes in a large pan of salted boiling water until tender, then pass them through a sieve into a bowl. Mix in the butter, cream and mustard and keep warm.

Serve the sausages with a good helping of the mash and a spoonful of warm onion marmalade.

3

AUTUMN

INTRODUCTION TO
AUTUMN

Having seen the frantic growth of spring and the maturing of summer, it is very apparent that winter is not far off, so autumn is the time to get your garden in order and harvest every last scrap of your bounty. The seed heads and berries are all looking at their best, and those not collected are gradually foraged for over the winter. If you want to make the most of your garden you have the opportunity now to make chutneys, pickles and jams, store your root vegetables and gradually move away from light summer salads to the comfort foods that are well suited to cold evenings. Use every opportunity to get into the garden to harvest regularly, though be wary of tramping over wet soil as it can adversely affect the soil's structure and take the air out of it; if necessary, lay down planks to walk on.

TIDYING

There is something very satisfying about tidying your plot so that you have months of neat beds ahead while the weather stops you getting outdoors. There are undoubtedly winter days when it is great to be out in the garden; however, walking over wet soil compacts it and adversely affects the structure by taking air out of it, so autumn is a good time to prepare your beds.

If you have a shortage of compost bins now is the time to build or get some new ones. As you tidy and weed for the last time this year you will generate lots of potential compost, and it's worth remembering that the goodness you put into your compost bins is saved and comes back to be used in future growing.

HELPING BEES & INSECTS

It pays to think of your allies when tidying up the garden. Ivy is one of the last flowering plants of the year and it is really important to

insects that need nectar, so think twice before savaging it. Plant fruit trees to provide early-season blossoms, and bulbs like snowdrops and crocuses, which are important for the early spring flights of the bees. If you are planting hedges to delineate your beds or boundaries, consider box and berberis, which will both provide early-season feeding for insects that can reduce the pests on your plot. Whole hedges of rosemary or bay are other good options and will provide you with an abundance of herbs.

There are numerous insects that are beneficial to the gardener. In winter they hibernate in crevices, under rocks at the base of trees or in garden refuse, where they are protected from the frost. For that reason it's worth leaving some areas specifically for the 'wildlife' to overwinter. Some creatures are allies to the gardener, such as frogs, toads, hedgehogs and ladybirds, and these will all be very happy to move into a strategically placed pile of leaves, rotten wood and rocks.

Everywhere you look, there are vegetables ready to be harvested

Lift any remaining carrots, ready to be clamped and stored

SAVING SEED

By now, any seed pods that you have left on your plants should have dried naturally and be papery and bone-dry. For more details of how to store them, see page 46.

PRUNING

Autumn is the time for getting out your secateurs to prune your fruit bushes, canes, and trees. The simple rule is to remove anything that is dead, damaged or diseased and any additional elements you need to get rid of to keep the desired shape.

FRUIT & NUT TREES

Mid to late autumn is the time to plant or move fruit and nut trees, specifically when the sap has stopped rising. Plant them in a hole that is bigger than the root ball and well manured. When you place the young tree in the hole, make sure the bark that was formerly at ground level is not planted any higher or lower in the new hole.

HARVESTING & STORING

There is nothing quite as satisfying as having your own produce stored and available when you are deciding what to have for a meal. Apart from preserving, which allows you to take a seasonal glut and transfer it to jars in the pantry, we obviously have fridges, freezers and a larder as fairly standard in most homes, but your opportunities are greatly enhanced if you have a store that is airy and frost-free.

Storing fresh produce is a skill that we have essentially lost, as supermarkets are constantly full of food from all over the world, but it is possible to take control of your food chain even in the dormant winter months. Our forebears had to be industrious in the autumn, and with a little effort you can accumulate a fairly significant amount of produce to enjoy.

Some crops, such as leeks, parsnips and swede, will happily sit out all winter; however, most of your produce will need to be harvested and brought in before the weather takes its toll. The first frost can ruin a crop so that the cellular structure breaks down and it cannot be stored so all your work to that point will have been wasted. Sort our your storerooms early and fill them in good time. Shelving and boxes need to be prepared in advance and a couple of days work will mean you have somewhere to place your crops. Our shelving has been up for years and we continually collect wooden boxes and cases to increase our storage capability.

AUTUMN TASKS

- Cut back any perennial plants that need it (generally those that flop over). Leave the upright ones to provide shelter for wildlife.
- Get on with pruning – there is a significant amount to be done.
- Dig over and manure any beds where you plan to make spring plantings of varieties that need significant nutrition.
- Remove all your canes, nets, stakes and tools, clean them and store them.
- There is still time for some successional planting in the greenhouse. It's also time to give it a good clean.
- Lift, divide and replant any overgrown herbaceous perennials.
- Pick up fallen fruit – don't leave it to rot on the ground.
- Collect fallen leaves to augment your compost heap.
- Pull up any dead annual plants in beds and compost them.
- Make sure to turn your compost.

METHOD #19

CHILLIES

When you imagine a garden full of vegetables, you may not be struck with excitement and raw passion. However, chillies are without a doubt the most exotic and fiery plant you can grow. The variety of chilli plants is astounding, and each type has not only its own distinct flavour but also a different degree of spicy heat or piquancy, which is measured according to the Scoville scale.

WHEN TO SOW	*late winter to early spring*
SOWING DEPTH	*1cm (½ inch)*
WHEN TO TRANSPLANT	*when seedlings are 2.5cm (1 inch) tall*
DISTANCE APART	*30–60cm (1–2 feet)*
WHEN TO HARVEST	*mid summer to mid autumn*
SUCCESSION PLANTING	*no*

SOW

Sow seeds indoors from late winter to early spring in small pots or seed trays. Sow to a depth of 1cm (½ inch), cover with fine compost and place in a heated propagator if you have one. If not, a plastic bag over the pot, held in place with an elastic band, will do.

GROW

When the seedlings are 2.5cm (1 inch) tall, transplant each one into its own 10cm (4 inch) pot and leave on a window sill or in a heated greenhouse. When your chillies are 20cm (8 inches) tall, support them with pea sticks or small canes. By early summer, when the plants have become more mature, you can move them outside. However, unlike many vegetables, they really do thrive in warm and humid conditions, so a greenhouse or polytunnel will give you the best results if your garden doesn't provide these conditions.

Pinch out the tips of the plants when they have reached about 30–40cm (1–1½ feet) tall. This will help the plants put energy into forming more branches, rather than becoming too stringy. When planting directly into the ground, leave a gap of 30–60cm (1–2 feet) between them and protect with cloches if there is any risk of frost.

Ready for the kitchen

COMPANION PLANTING

Chillies benefit from high humidity levels, so plant dense ground-covering herbs, such as basil, oregano and marjoram, beneath them to help keep the moisture around the plants.

PESTS & DISEASES

Grey mould, or botrytis, is a fungal disease that can ruin your chilli crops and eventually kill the plants. It thrives in high humidity levels, so leave enough of a gap between plants and ventilate your greenhouse every day to allow air to circulate around your plants.

Whitefly are another nuisance – they will suck the sap from your plant. If you are growing your chillies in an enclosed space, it's worth using a biological control. A tiny parasitic wasp called *Encarsia formosa* (available online) will do the trick!

HARVEST

Using scissors or secateurs, cut the chillies often from mid summer onwards.

STORE

Harvest chillies at regular intervals until near the end of the season. After that, it's best to allow to ripen fully on the plant. The colours and flavours will intensify, making them more suitable for storage. Fresh chillies can be kept for a couple of weeks in the fridge. For the long term, make strings of chillies and hang them in an airy place away from any rain to dry. When they are completely dry, store in a glass jar somewhere cool and dark.

EAT

Chilli can transform a dish. When adding chilli, consider experimenting with balancing the hot, the sweet and the sour: add sugar or honey, and vinegar, lemon juice or lime juice.

THE SCOVILLE SCALE

HEAT RATING	CHILLIES
over 1,000,000	Bhut Jolokia
100,000–350,000	Scotch Bonnet, Habanero
50,000–100,000	Bird's Eye
30,000–50,000	Cayenne, Tabasco
10,000–23,000	Serrano
3,500–8,000	Jalapeño
1,000–2,500	Poblano, Rocotillo, Peppadew
100–900	Pimento, Banana Pepper
0	Bell Peppers

You may feel daunted the first time you cook squid, but it is not difficult, and once you've tasted it you'll be coming back for more. The chilli and tomato go together really well -- the sweetness and heat will bring your tastebuds to life.

SERVES 4

500g (1lb) baby squid, gutted

1 tablespoon extra virgin olive oil

1 garlic clove, crushed

4 fresh red chillies, sliced

6 tomatoes, diced

1 glass of white wine

3 tablespoons chopped fresh coriander

salt and freshly ground black pepper

fresh bread, to serve

CHILLI SQUID

First, prepare the squid. Cut the bodies into rings and leave the tentacles whole if they are small; or cut them up if large. Dry with kitchen paper.

Heat the olive oil in a large frying pan. When the oil is hot, throw in the squid and toss vigorously. Cook for about a minute, then add the garlic and toss. Add the chillies and toss again, then add the tomatoes and give them a final toss. Cook for about a minute, then add the wine and simmer for a further 2 minutes.

Finally, add the coriander and season with salt and pepper, then serve with fresh bread.

METHOD #20

FENNEL

Fennel is a vegetable with a distinctive aniseed taste. The bulbs, fronds, seeds and even the stalks can be eaten, and all have the aniseed flavour. Fennel originates from the Mediterranean so it does like a bit of sunshine, but it is possible to grow it very successfully in cooler climates.

SOW

Fennel can be grown from seed or by dividing the roots. The seeds are slow to germinate, so in early spring it is best to sow them under cover and only try sowing outside after all danger of frost has passed. Fennel does not like being transplanted, so it is best to sow the seeds in compostable pots, or try toilet rolls packed with compost. Don't plant fennel near dill, as cross-fertilization may occur. Fennel and tomatoes or potatoes do not do well if planted near each other.

Sow the fennel in rows 45cm (18 inches) apart and 1cm (½ inch) deep, covering the seeds with a fine tilth. The plants can easily grow to 1m (about 3 feet) high, so they need reasonable separation. Covering the beds with black plastic to keep them warm is useful for early sowings. You can succession sow every couple of weeks.

For division, split fennel vertically and plant the segments in sandy soil in the autumn, for maturing the following year.

GROW

If sown in situ, thin out plants so they are about 30cm (1 foot) apart. Fennel requires regular watering in dry periods, and you need to keep weeds down in the beds. When the bulbs start to form, and are about 4cm (1½ inches) across, bring the surrounding soil up to cover the bulbs, which will ensure they keep their white colour. Within the month, the fennel should be ready for harvesting.

SAVING SEEDS

If the plant bolts and goes to seed, the seeds can also be used. When they are ripe, cut off the seed heads and bunch several together, then put the heads inside a paper bag with the stalks sticking out. They can then be hung in the kitchen or in a dry, airy place. When the

WHEN TO SOW	*early spring to mid summer*
SOWING DEPTH	*1cm (½ inch)*
DISTANCE APART	*rows 45cm (18 inches), thin seedlings to 30cm (1 foot)*
WHEN TO TRANSPLANT	*when 10cm (4 inches) tall*
WHEN TO HARVEST	*mid summer to mid autumn*
SUCCESSION PLANTING	*yes*

EAT

Tender fennel stalks and bulbs can be thinly sliced and added to salad. Braising brings out the fresh yet rich flavour of the bulbs.

seeds are dry, store them in airtight containers and either use them in your cooking or keep them to sow next season.

PESTS & DISEASES

Fennel does not suffer from significant insect and disease problems, but watch out for greenfly in the foliage and for slug or snail damage to the seedlings. Weeding in the early stages of growth is essential.

HARVEST

Fennel fronds and stems can be harvested young, as and when you need them. The bulbs can stay in the ground and be harvested from mid summer to mid autumn.

STORE

Keep fennel in the ground and dig it up as required. It can also be blanched and then frozen. Dry the seeds and fronds by hanging the flowers upside down in a brown paper envelope. Fennel bulbs can be crystallized in segments, just like candied citrus peel.

A perfect bulb ↗

Fennel is one of those superstar vegetables that are special because all their components taste good: seeds, bulbs, leaves and stalks. We love serving it thinly sliced as a salad, and using the seeds to flavour chorizo sausages or sweet potato mash, but to really release fennel's flavours you can't beat roasting it.

SERVES 4

2 fennel bulbs, plus the green fronds
50g (2oz) butter, melted
100ml (3½ fl oz) white wine
150g (5oz) chestnuts
salt and freshly ground black pepper
175g (6oz) blue cheese, crumbled

FOR THE APPLE CHUTNEY

2 apples
1 tablespoon sugar
1 tablespoon Calvados
1 tablespoon raisins
1 tablespoon cider vinegar

ROASTED FENNEL WITH BLUE CHEESE & CHESTNUTS

To make the apple chutney, cut the apples into 1cm (½ inch) cubes and put them into a small pan over a medium heat with the sugar and Calvados. Flambé the apple: use a long match to carefully set the alcohol alight at the edge of the pan and let it burn off. When the flames have died down, add the raisins and vinegar. Stir until the apples have softened, then cook for a further 15 minutes until the chutney has reduced and thickened. After 15 minutes turn off the heat, spoon into a small sterilized jar and leave to cool.

Preheat the oven to 180°C (350°F), Gas Mark 4. Cut the fennel bulbs into segments and place in a pan. Add the melted butter and white wine and cook over a medium heat on the stove for 5–10 minutes, or until the fennel starts to soften. Add the chestnuts, season generously with salt and pepper and mix together.

Transfer the fennel and chestnut mixture to an ovenproof dish and bake in the oven for 15 minutes, then remove and top with the blue cheese. Put back into the oven for a further 3–4 minutes, or until the cheese starts to melt.

Serve with the fresh apple chutney.

METHOD #21

CARROTS

Eating vast quantities of carrots won't in fact improve your eyesight, but these root vegetables are packed with vitamins and absolutely delicious. You can cook and serve carrots in a multitude of different ways, and they don't even necessarily have to be organge -- you can grow purple, yellow and white varieties, too. They can be short, medium or long: the short-rooted types are the easiest ones to grow, as they mature quickly and are more forgiving of the soil conditions.

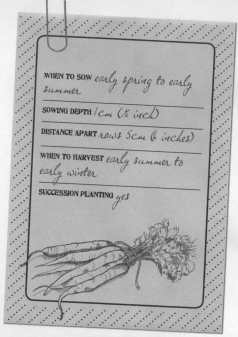

WHEN TO SOW *early spring to early summer*

SOWING DEPTH *1cm (½ inch)*

DISTANCE APART *rows 5cm (6 inches)*

WHEN TO HARVEST *early summer to early winter*

SUCCESSION PLANTING *yes*

SOW

Carrots like deep, fertile soil that has not been recently manured. It's best not to try growing carrots in areas where fertilizer has been added to the soil in the last year, as the resulting crop will be misshapen. Work the soil well before sowing the seeds in rows 15cm (6 inches) apart, in spring and early summer, and sow very thinly, about 1cm (½ inch) down. To help you sow thinly, mix the seeds with fine sand.

GROW

Thin out the seedlings when they are large enough to handle, leaving enough space between plants for the carrots to grow to maturity.

When the carrots are very young, weed between the rows, but once the plants are established it is best to let the dense leaves do the job of depriving any weeds of light and thereby controlling them. Water carrots

regularly in dry periods, as inconsistent watering can cause the carrots to split.

PESTS & DISEASES

Carrot fly can be an issue, so make sure you remove your thinnings, and be aware that the smell of the bruised foliage can actually attract the flies, so thin carefully. Planting carrots near onions, garlic and other alliums will deter carrot fly.

HARVEST

When the carrots reach the desired size, dig them out with a fork. Remember that the smaller the carrot the sweeter the taste. In autumn, lift all remaining carrots for storage. Only sound vegetables should be stored.

STORE

Carrots can be kept in the fridge, or blanched for 5 minutes then frozen, but the best way to store them is to make a clamp, which is a method that can be used for other root vegetables as well. To make a clamp, drill several holes in the base of a bucket. Spread an 8cm (3 inch) layer of sawdust in the bottom of the bucket, followed by a single layer of carrots. Cover and repeat until the layers fill the bucket. Then dig a hole in the ground and fill the base with a few stones. Place the bucket in the hole and cover with a 27cm (10–11 inch) thick layer of straw and then a 5cm (2 inch) layer of earth. Alternatively, you can store the bucket with its straw and earth mulch, uncovered, in a cellar or cool shed.

EAT

Their sweet flavour, crunchy texture and vivid colours make carrots popular and very versatile. Enjoy them raw in salads or cut into batons as crudités, pickled or turned into a delicious and healthy juice. Diced carrots add depth of flavour and colour to soups and broths, can be grated into sauces to add sweetness and are also delicious roasted with a little honey. Toss lightly boiled carrots in butter or cook them until soft and mash them with swede or parsnips. Carrots can even form the basis of a delicious cake, so why not try turning them into a tea-time treat?

Instant plant pots ➚

Carrot soup is sweet, delicious and very economical. We use caraway to add a slightly exotic fragrance to the dish, but you could substitute cumin seed for the caraway if you prefer.

SERVES 4

750g (1½lb) carrots

25g (1oz) butter

2 garlic cloves, chopped

2 teaspoons caraway seeds

500ml (17fl oz) vegetable or chicken stock

200ml (7fl oz) orange juice

salt and freshly ground black pepper

crème fraîche, to serve

CARROT & CARAWAY SOUP

Top and tail the carrots, then cut them into 2.5cm (1 inch) chunks.

Melt the butter in a pan. Throw in the carrots, garlic and half the caraway seeds and fry gently for about 5 minutes. Add the stock and orange juice, bring to the boil, then reduce the heat and leave to simmer for about 15 minutes.

Whizz the soup in a blender or food processor, then return it to the pan. Add the remaining caraway seeds and simmer for another 10 minutes, then taste and add salt if necessary.

Serve the carrot soup with a dollop of crème fraîche and a twist of black pepper.

WINTER SQUASHES

There is something very special about growing winter squashes, as the results tend to be impressive, with their different colours, shapes and textures. Children (of all ages!) love the competition of growing giant squashes. The seeds grow quickly and there is a real sense of achievement that can culminate in truly magnificent pumpkins. There are two basic types of squash: summer and winter. Winter squashes are much slower growing than summer varieties such as courgettes, and tend to take longer to mature. Some squashes grow on long vines and are great for storing, as they have thick skins. Examples are butternut squash, acorn squash and pumpkins. We like to grow a crop and store them so that we can enjoy squash soup right through the winter.

SOW

All squashes are vulnerable to frosts. To start growing them early, they can be sown under glass but the seedlings cannot be planted out until well after any frost threat has passed.

Sow the seeds in rich compost in reasonable-sized pots (10 cm/4 inches) and transplant out when there are at least 2 true leaves (the small round cotyledon – the first 2 leaves to emerge from the seed – don't count).

WHEN TO SOW *mid spring to early summer*

SOWING DEPTH *2cm (¾ inch)*

WHEN TO TRANSPLANT *when all risk of frost has passed*

DISTANCE APART *60cm (2 feet)*

WHEN TO HARVEST *late summer to mid autumn*

SUCCESSION PLANTING *no*

GROW

Squash plants have large leaves and require soil that has been well manured and is rich in organic matter. To allow for good drainage,

plant your squash on a mound of soil. If you dig a hole and fill it with compost, the resulting mound made when the dug-out soil is put back is perfect.

Squash don't require regular watering, so follow the no-water policy (see page 46): give them one good dose of water when you plant them out, then leave them on their own.

SAVING SEED

If you want to save your seeds, you need to avoid cross-pollinations. Only plant a single variety to keep the seeds pure, or separate the different types of squash by a distance of more than 200m (650 feet).

HARVEST

A squash or pumpkin is ready to store when the skin is hard enough to withstand the imprint of your fingernail and when the stem connecting the fruit to the plant is shrivelled up and dry. Harvest your squashes before the first frost, so that they are in optimum condition for storage. If the stalks are broken off, use these squashes first to avoid rot. Otherwise, cut the stalks about 5cm (2 inches) from the body of the squash. Finally, be gentle with your squashes – some will be heavy, but set them down gently to avoid bruising.

STORE

Store your winter squashes in a dry, well-ventilated area and make sure they don't touch each other.

EAT

Roasted with garlic, chilli and olive oil, squash makes a great accompaniment to a meat dish. You can also add stock to roast squash to make a quick, hearty soup.

Harvest with care

Gnocchi are usually made with potatoes, but squash makes an excellent substitute and the results are fantastic. We've made it with butternut, but you can use any squash you have to hand for this recipe.

SERVES 4

1kg (2lb) butternut squash (or any variety), peeled and cut into 4cm (1½ inch) cubes

3 garlic cloves

extra virgin olive oil

salt and freshly ground black pepper

a pinch of grated nutmeg

1 egg, beaten

150g (5oz) Parmesan cheese, grated

5 tablespoons plain flour

150g (5oz) butter

10 fresh sage leaves

BUTTERNUT SQUASH GNOCCHI

Preheat the oven to 200°C (400°F), Gas Mark 6.

Put the squash on a baking sheet with 2 of the garlic cloves. Drizzle with extra virgin olive oil and cook in the oven for about 40 minutes, until soft. Force the squash and garlic through a sieve into a bowl, then set aside to cool. Season with salt.

Mix the squash with the nutmeg, egg, cheese and flour, adding a little more flour if the mixture is too soft. Roll the dough into a sausage about 2.5cm (1 inch) thick, then cut it into pieces about 2.5cm (1 inch) long. Use a fork to press the pieces into flatter gnocchi shapes.

Bring a large pan of salted water to the boil and drop batches of the gnocchi into the water. When they float to the top, continue to simmer for about 1 minute before fishing them out and draining well. Keep warm while you cook the rest.

To serve, melt the butter in a frying pan. Chop the remaining garlic clove and add to the pan with the sage leaves. Cook for 3 minutes, then toss the gnocchi in the flavoured butter and serve with black pepper.

Press gnocchi into shape

METHOD #23

CELERIAC

Celeriac is a plant with a large turnip-shaped root that tastes of celery. This is not surprising, as celery and celeriac have their origins in the same wild plant. Celeriac makes great eating, raw or cooked, and it keeps really well in a root cellar or clamp. It is easy to grow small celeriac, but you need to give it a little attention to achieve the size that will feed a family. The flavour and texture of celeriac remain unchanged even as it grows larger, so the bigger the better.

WHEN TO SOW *early spring*

SOWING DEPTH *5mm (¼ inch)*

WHEN TO TRANSPLANT *early summer*

DISTANCE APART *plants 30cm (1 foot), rows 45cm (18 inches)*

WHEN TO HARVEST *late autumn to early winter*

SUCCESSION PLANTING *no*

SOW

Sow celeriac seeds in compost-filled pots in early spring. Sow 2 seeds to each pot and remove the weaker seedling when they start growing. Germination can be erratic, so always sow more than you intend to use. You will make someone happy by passing on the surplus seedlings.

GROW

Harden the seedlings off (see page 17) before transplanting them outside after the last risk of frost. Celeriac likes soil that retains some moisture and the more fertile the better, so dig in some manure in the autumn.

Plant the seedlings 30cm (1 foot) apart in rows separated by 45cm (18 inches). Ensure the base of the stem is planted at ground level and the soil is firmly pressed in around the seedling. Water the seedlings in well after planting.

There are numerous varieties of celeriac, and it is worth going for a large one, plus a medium-sized, strong-flavoured variety.

You will need to hoe between the rows to keep the weeds down and mulch to retain moisture. Trim any side shoots off the celeriac, and from mid summer onwards trim the leaves as well, cutting off the lower leaves so that the sun reaches the root.

PESTS & DISEASES

Celeriac suffers from few serious pest problems, so it's a good vegetable for the organic gardener. However, it does not compete well with weeds, so tend the drills well, taking care not to disturb the shallow roots.

HARVEST

It is possible to leave celeriac in the ground over winter. If you do this, your crops will benefit from being covered with straw.

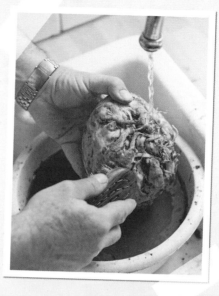

Otherwise, begin to harvest in late autumn. When you dig them up, just trim off the roots with a sharp knife and and cut or twist off the stems about 3 cm (1¼ inches) above the celeriac.

STORE

Celeriac can be stored in a cool, dark root cellar, in a clamp (see page 121) or in a bucket filled with damp sand. Celeriac will keep in the fridge for up to 2 weeks. If you want to freeze celeriac, cut it into cubes and blanch it for 3 minutes first.

EAT

Celeriac discolours very quickly once cut, so you will have to toss it in lemon juice or a dressing if you want to serve it raw, for example as a classic French celeriac remoulade. Grated celeriac can also be made into a crispy rosti. Celeriac makes a wonderful mash – if you add some horseradish, it is a particularly good accompaniment for roast beef.

Trim off all the stalks

We like to eat celeriac both raw and cooked. This soup is quick and easy to make – in fact, it can be made in less time than a trip to the supermarket to buy a ready-made soup.

SERVES 4

2 medium celeriac

50g (2oz) butter

1 onion, chopped

2 garlic cloves, finely chopped

500ml (17fl oz) vegetable or chicken stock

200g (7oz) creamy blue cheese, such as Stilton

500ml (17fl oz) milk

200ml (7fl oz) cream (optional)

salt and freshly ground black pepper

FOR THE GARLIC CROUTONS

2 tablespoons extra virgin olive oil

1 garlic clove, crushed

a pinch of rock salt or sea salt

4 slices of stale bread, cut into cubes

CELERIAC & BLUE CHEESE SOUP

Peel the celeriac and cut it into 1cm (½ inch) dice. Melt the butter in a large pan, then add the celeriac, onion and garlic and cook for about 5 minutes, until softened but not coloured. Add the stock and bring to the boil, then reduce the heat and simmer until the celeriac is tender.

Meanwhile, make the garlic croutons. Heat the extra virgin olive oil in a frying pan and add the garlic and salt. Add the bread cubes and fry until golden brown, then set aside to drain on kitchen paper.

When the celeriac is cooked, crumble in the cheese and when it's melted, add the milk and cream. Let the soup cool down a bit, then blend until smooth. Season with salt and pepper and add more cream if you want a richer soup.

Serve the soup with the garlic croutons scattered on top.

KOHLRABI

Kohlrabi may look like a mutant vegetable from another planet but it is actually a fairly normal brassica that grows extremely easily. One of the great things about it is that it matures quickly and is relatively problem-free. There are two main varieties: white (or light green) and purple. Both taste great, so grow a single variety or a colourful combination in your garden.

SOW

You can sow your kohlrabi from late winter onwards if you are using a cloche or seed trays under cover. Sow seeds in small batches but often, to provide yourself with a steady supply of kohlrabi. Scatter the seed thinly in rows 30cm (1 foot) apart, covering them with 1cm (½ inch) of compost.

GROW

Thin out the seedlings when they are around 5cm (2 inches) tall and have formed proper leaves, to leave about 15cm (6 inches) between each plant. If you are transplanting them outside from trays, wait until early to mid spring and harden the seedlings off during the day – putting them outside and bringing them back inside each evening.

Watering and weeding are important for young plants. If there hasn't been much rain and you are worried about your kohlrabi drying out, try to keep them shaded from the sun by heaping grass cuttings or mulch around them. This will also prevent them becoming too woody in texture.

PESTS & DISEASES

One key job that you have to take seriously is netting. Young brassica seedlings are very attractive to pigeons and they will devastate your crops if you don't protect them.

HARVEST

Don't wait until your kohlrabi are huge or they may be tough, fibrous and bland. Instead, try to pick them – especially the white varieties – when the bulbs are about the size of a tennis ball. Some of the purple-

Hardening off

WHEN TO SOW *late winter to late spring*

SOWING DEPTH *1 cm (½ inch)*

DISTANCE APART *rows 30cm (1 foot), thin seedlings to 15cm (6 inches)*

WHEN TO TRANSPLANT *early to mid spring*

WHEN TO HARVEST *early summer to mid winter*

SUCCESSION PLANTING *yes*

skinned varieties can grow very large without developing this toughness, so it's safe to leave them to grow.

STORE

To store your kohlrabi, remove the leaves and set aside any that have damaged roots or diseased patches. If you are aiming to keep kohlrabi for longer than a week in the fridge, the best option is to keep them moist. Either wrap them in a damp towel or store them in a clamp with moist sand (see page 121). Alternatively, cut them in half, blanch them and freeze for long-term storage.

EAT

Kohlrabi tastes like a cross between cabbage and celery, and has a nutty quality. Trim off the stems and ends and peel the bulb like a potato. Try it both raw and cooked – it is best to keep it a little 'al dente'. You can eat the leaves too: they are good sautéed with butter and garlic.

Purple Kohlrabi ↗

Coleslaw is very versatile – it's great on its own or served with sandwiches, and it can accompany most meats. This version is great for a barbecue and the apple makes it particularly good with pork sausages. You can chop the ingredients by hand, but a mandolin slicer makes this salad very quick to prepare.

SERVES 4

4 carrots

2 kohlrabi

2 apples

2 tablespoons mayonnaise

zest and juice of 1 lime

KOHLRABI COLESLAW

Peel the carrots and kohlrabi and cut them into matchsticks. Pop them into a bowl.

Next, peel and cut the apples to match. Put them into the bowl, then add the mayonnaise, lime zest and juice and toss well to coat. Serve immediately.

METHOD #25

HORSERADISH

It was only relatively recently that we started to grow our own horseradish. It took us ages to source the root, but now we have masses and all our friends, relatives and acquaintances have more than they will ever need. Therein lies the gift and curse of growing horseradish -- it needs to be kept under control. Now that we have an abundant supply it is something that we would never be without in our garden. It's very easy to grow, and once you've tasted fresh horseradish you cannot go back to the shop-bought version.

PLANT

In early spring make a hole in the ground with a dibber, about 15cm (6 inches) deep, and pop in a root fragment.

Horseradish can be invasive. To stop it from spreading, you can treat it a bit like mint, burying buckets with the bottoms cut out of them in the ground and planting the roots

inside. If you do this you need to harvest significant amounts annually, otherwise the roots will grow and can cause the bucket to split.

Plant horseradish in a permanent bed: while it is possible to dig out all the roots in the autumn and replant them again the following year, any root fragments left in the soil will grow again. Another option is to plant the roots in dustbins full of compost – all you need to do in the autumn is tip the contents out, harvest what you need and then replant for the following year.

GROW

Keep the area weed-free until the large leaves grow. Once horseradish has produced its large, robust leaves, there is very little you have to do for it. All plants like a little water in times of drought, obviously, but horseradish is a plant that you can actually forget about until it's time to harvest.

PESTS & DISEASES

Horseradish is very resilient and doesn't really suffer from serious pests and diseases. Some caterpillars may start to eat at the leaves,

WHEN TO PLANT	*early spring*
PLANTING DEPTH	*15cm (6 inches)*
DISTANCE APART	*45cm (18 inches)*
WHEN TO HARVEST	*year round*
SUCCESSION PLANTING	*no*

A little goes a long way

which can become a bit lacey as a result, but the roots will not be seriously affected.

HARVEST

You can use your horseradish throughout the year, pulling up a root whenever you need one (this is when roots grown in containers are particulalry handy, as they come out very easily), but it is in the autumn that the crop should be harvested and the roots should be dug out.

When someone tells you to 'dig out the roots', you may be forgiven for thinking that all you do is pop the fork in the ground and ease the root out. Not so. The roots are impressive and you may need an extra-strong fork. Be prepared for some of the roots to snap, hence the logic of having a permanent bed – if you wish to move the crop you will have to get out every root fragment.

STORE

The roots can be stored in sand over winter for regular use and to keep for spring planting. Peeled horseradish can also be grated and put into jars with oil or vinegar for convenience. Note that grating horseradish will make your eyes water – the easiest thing to do is to use the shredder attachment of a food processor.

EAT

You can preserve horseradish as a paste: put 225g (7½oz) of peeled and cubed horseradish root, 175ml (6fl oz) of distilled cider vinegar, 2 teaspoons of caster sugar and ¼ teaspoon of salt into a blender and whizz to a paste. Pop into a sterilized jar and store in the fridge. The horseradish will lose a little of its heat over time, so be prepared to use more than you think you'll need. It's delicious with smoked mackerel, roast beef and sausages.

These little appetizers really get the tastebuds going before dinner – there is horseradish in both the biscuit base and the sauce. They are a little fiddly to make, but it's worth the work, as they are absolutely delicious.

SERVES 4

100g (3½ oz) plain flour

4 tablespoons icing sugar

1 teaspoon salt

100g (3½ oz) butter, very soft

2 egg whites

about 25g (1oz) finely grated horseradish

225g (7½ oz) beef fillet, trimmed of fat

salt and freshly ground black pepper

sunflower oil, for brushing

FOR THE HORSERADISH SAUCE

2 teaspoons grated horseradish

juice of ½ a lemon

100ml (3½ fl oz) double cream, lightly whipped

a pinch of sugar

a pinch of English mustard powder

HORSERADISH & BEEF BITES

To make the horseradish sauce, mix all the ingredients together in a bowl and store in a jar in the fridge, where it will keep for up to 3 weeks. If you prefer a mild horseradish, soak the grated horseradish in hot water for 10 minutes, then strain and combine with the rest of the ingredients.

Preheat the oven to 200°C (400°F), Gas Mark 6, and line a large baking sheet with non-stick baking parchment or a silicone sheet.

Mix the flour, icing sugar and salt in a bowl. Gradually beat in the butter, about a third at a time.

Whisk the 2 egg whites in a separate bowl until soft peaks form when the whisk is removed. Mix half the egg white into the butter mixture, then fold in the remainder along with the horseradish.

Spread the mixture in a thin layer on the baking sheet and bake in the oven for about 8–10 minutes, or until pale golden brown. Allow to cool for a couple of minutes, then, using a pastry cutter, cut it into circles. Before they harden, shape them into crumpled bowls.

Wrap the beef in clingfilm and put it into the freezer for 45 minutes. Heat a griddle until searing hot. Using a very sharp knife, cut the beef across the grain into small squares. Season with salt and pepper, brush with a little sunflower oil and sear for 1 minute on each side.

Crumple the beef into small rolls and stuff one inside each biscuit bowl. Top with a dollop of horseradish sauce.

METHOD #26

SWEET POTATO

We've been enjoying sweet potatoes for years but we've only recently begun growing them in the garden. Sweet potato is a delicious crop that is easy to grow if you choose one of the hardier varieties. If you have a sunny, sheltered garden why not have a go – they have more vitamin C than the classic potato and are great fun to cook.

WHEN TO PLANT *late spring*

PLANTING DEPTH *5cm (2 inches)*

DISTANCE APART *slips 30cm (1 foot), rows 45cm (18 inches)*

WHEN TO TRANSPLANT *late spring to early summer*

WHEN TO HARVEST *autumn*

SUCCESSION PLANTING *no*

PLANT

The easiest way to grow sweet potatoes is to buy 'slips' (available by mail order) and plant them 30cm (1 foot) apart and 5cm (2 inches) deep. They will provide ground cover all summer and a harvest of tubers. You can also grow them from tubers that you plant into a pot or tray filled with moist soil mixed with a third of its volume of sand and then allow to sprout in an airing cupboard or a warm propagator. Similar to chitting potatoes, this job is vital to the success of your crop.

GROW

Once your sweet potatoes have produced shoots a few inches long, cut away the pieces of tuber with the sprouts on them with a sharp knife and plant the chunks with sprouts into small pots of cutting compost (a mixture of equal parts sharp sand and good compost). Keep them moist and place a clear plastic bag over each pot and secure it with an elastic band as a mini-propagator.

Harden off your sweet potatoes before planting them in warm soil. This can mean waiting until late spring and early summer before planting them outside, but you can bring your season forward by warming up the ground beforehand – cover it with black plastic in early to mid spring. Growing them through plastic will also make the individual plants easier to locate when the tubers are ready to harvest. For best results, grow sweet potatoes in a large pot in the greenhouse.

Protect sweet potato plants with fleece if there is any chance of a cold spell as they will not tolerate frost. They like well-drained soil, so the key thing that you can do to increase your chances of a good crop is to start with rich soil that has been well dug over.

If you are growing them under cover, spray the plants with water every week to keep them from getting dry, which makes them more susceptible to pests.

Protected by plastic

PESTS & DISEASES

Red spider mite and whitefly are the main problems for sweet potatoes grown in a greenhouse, but these pests can easily be treated with a commercial spray.

HARVEST

Wait until the foliage dies back or turns yellow before lifting the sweet potatoes. This can take up to 5 months, but it'll be worth the wait.

STORE

Sweet pototaes are best consumed within a few days of harvesting. Stored in a cool, dark place, they will keep for up to 10 days.

EAT

Sweet potatoes are tasty and versatile – you can try anything you would do with a standard spud, but the results will be softer. Scrubbed, pricked all over and roasted, they are particularly good with a sharper filling to complement their sweetness. To make sweet potato chips, fry once, allow to cool, then coat in seasoned flour prior to the second frying.

Our favourite sweet potato recipe is this baked pie with fennel seeds and plenty of goats' cheese. It's an easy meal to make in a hurry and guaranteed to please vegetarian guests.

BAKED SWEET POTATO & GOATS' CHEESE PIE

Preheat the oven to 180°C (350°F), Gas Mark 4.

Heat half the butter in a small pan and add the garlic and shallots. Cook gently until softened, then add the spinach and nutmeg and give it a final stir on the heat. Transfer to a sieve and drain, so that the spinach isn't too watery when used later.

Bring a large pan of salted water to the boil, then add the sweet potatoes and cook for about 20 minutes, or until mashable. Add the rest of the butter and the fennel seeds, season with salt and mash until smooth.

Now layer half the sweet potato mash in the bottom of a pie dish, with the drained spinach on top. Spread over the goats' cheese, then top with the remaining sweet potato.

Sprinkle the nuts and seed evenly over the top of the dish and bake in the oven for 5–10 minutes.

4

WINTER

INTRODUCTION TO

WINTER

If you think that winter in your garden will be a time of hibernation and rest, you are sadly mistaken. We find it one of the most physically demanding times of the year. There is not as much growing in the ground, and it is a period when the soil can have a dormant feel to it, a feeling of rest before spring. However, there are plenty of jobs to be done, and the clearing, conditioning and preparation of the vegetable patch is a job in itself. We also use winter to maintain our tools and gardening equipment and plan the next growing cycle.

PLANNING

Deciding what to grow where is a good job for the start of a new year. Growing the same crops in the same place every time will increase the risk of disease and exhaust the soil, so we divide our beds into 4 vegetable families – brassicas, alliums, legumes and umbellifers – and rotate them regularly.

DIGGING

Frost does a great job of breaking up the soil in your vegetable beds into a fine tilth (a crumbly texture), but we find it is still well worth digging the beds one more time before spring sowing. Not only does it help the soil structure, but it also unearths any sleeping pests and exposes them to hungry birds. Try to use a scaffolding plank to walk on in the garden so that you don't compact the soil.

NURTURING THE SOIL

Providing your crops with appropriate soil conditions is the key to a successful kitchen garden. It's good gardening practice to think of the soil structure as the foundation of a productive plot.

Topping up raised beds and dressing the tops of plant pots with our homemade compost, which has been breaking down over the autumn, is a rewarding and vital job, replenishing all the used nutrients and preparing beds for a thriving spring. For us, the job involves turning all the compost, removing what's ready to use and putting the rest back into the compost bin again to give it a bit more time. It is at this point that we add activators such as freshly scythed nettles and grass cuttings (see page 21). In addition, we lime the beds that will be planted with brassicas.

COMPOST TRENCHES

Compost trenches are a really good alternative to a normal compost heap. They are particularly useful over the winter months, when conventional compost bins have cooled down. Simply choose a patch in a vegetable plot that will have runner beans or peas growing in it over the next season. During the winter, dig a trench one spade deep and a spade's width across. The key is to fill it gradually with vegetable scraps and kitchen waste, covering this with the

Harvest your parsnips when the green leaves have died back

Curly Kale is good for you and goes well with stews and casseroles

removed soil from the trench as you go along. After the whole of the trench is filled, leave it for a couple of months and then either sow seeds or plant directly into it. The advantage of a compost trench is that it is a great source of food for young plants, with the organic material providing a rich supply of nutrients to the roots. Grow rows of early peas along the trench in spring, or plant courgettes once the risk of frost has passed.

CLOCHES AND COLD FRAMES

In winter, position cloches and cold frames outside on the vegetable beds to warm up the ground before planting in the spring. You can also use large sheets of black plastic, which will dramatically bring forward your spring growing season.

CLEANING

Spring-cleaning the polytunnel and greenhouse has become a poultry-inspired ritual for us. We allow our chickens to live in the polytunnel for a few days to eat any fallen or diseased fruit and find any sleeping pests and grubs that could cause damage later in the season. It is a great low-effort way to clean under cover before getting stuck in with fresh compost for the raised beds and cleaning out any stored plant pots and trays.

TOOLS

'He that would perfect his work must first sharpen his tools' – Confucius must have been a gardener! Sharpening scythes, hoes and axes is a lovely way to stay warm, and shiny blades are their own reward. Winter is also the perfect time to clean your tools and put them away carefully, ready for spring.

COOKING WINTER PRODUCE

Winter tends to be a time for one-pot cooking, be it on the hob or in the oven, and most winter produce does well when cooked in this way. Traditionally, the dark, cold days of winter are when people tend to cook heavy dishes with lots of calories to provide them with energy to keep warm, and full. Most of our recipes deliberately take you away from that mind-set by making you consider things other than stews and casseroles.

WINTER TASKS

- Protect fragile plants with fleece, straw, a cloche or a cold frame.
- Build garden structures such as raised beds or greenhouses while you have the time.
- Clean out old pots and containers.
- Brush down trays and propagators and clean greenhouse glass.
- Harvest the last of your leeks and brassicas.
- Chit potatoes, so that you get to enjoy some early spuds as soon as possible!
- To reduce the chances of disease, compost or burn old crops instead of leaving them to decay on your vegetable beds.
- Prune back any trees that may be shading your plot.
- Condition your soil.
- Feed the birds.
- Harden seedlings off gradually and wait until frost-risk is reduced before planting them out.
- Turn off your irrigation system, otherwise it may freeze and break at a time when your plants don't even need extra watering.
- Always check bonfires for hibernating hedgehogs before setting them alight – they are gardening allies that love to eat slugs!

WILD ROCKET

Wild rocket can grow all year round, whereas conventional rocket, its domesticated relation, is an annual plant and therefore needs replacing after each crop. There are also differences in appearance and taste: the darker, serrated leaves of wild rocket have a slightly more intense pepper taste. Wild rocket can be used at any time of year to add a mustardy quality to salads and pizzas, but its fresh leaves are particularly welcome in the winter months.

SOW

Wild rocket seeds can be sown between early spring and late summer in thin drills. Sow them in full sun to a depth of 1cm (½ inch). Keep the rows at least 30cm (1 foot) apart. Perennial and wild rocket can be grown from seeds in the same way as annual rocket, but it can also be grown from cuttings.

GROW

Thin the seedlings so that there is 20–25cm (8–10 inches) space between plants – and

eat the plants you thin out as a healthy snack. To prevent the rocket from bolting (going to seed), try to prevent the soil getting too dry. If it is extremely hot and sunny you could use a shade umbrella to reduce the direct sunlight. By the end of its first year your rocket plants shouldn't need much protection from the winter elements. However, if they are planted outside, using a cold frame means you can enjoy harvesting rocket into the colder months. Under cover you will be astounded at the vitality and pungent flavour of the plant. Once it starts to flower you can either extend the season by picking the flowers or let them go to seed. The flowers are quite tasty added to salads, so why not try picking some during the first part of the season and then allow them to set seed in the latter part?

You can increase your number of rocket plants by taking your own cuttings: simply cut stems and root them in fine compost. Another option is to split the root clumps, re-pot them and bring them indoors for easy access.

PESTS & DISEASES

Rocket tends to be robust, but flea beetles can be a problem -- treat them as you would for radishes (see page 59).

← *Rocket can be very peppery*

WHEN TO SOW	*early spring to late summer*
SOWING DEPTH	*1cm (½ inch)*
DISTANCE APART	*rows 30cm (1 foot), thin seedlings to 20–25cm (8–10 inches)*
WHEN TO TRANSPLANT	*when the seedlings are large enough to handle*
WHEN TO HARVEST	*year round*
SUCCESSION PLANTING	*yes*

HARVEST

Harvest the rocket by cutting the leaves off with scissors or stripping leaves by hand. Treat it as a cut-and-come-again crop – the more you pick, the fresher and more tender the leaves that grow back will be. You can cut rocket back to 5cm (2 inches) and it will grow again.

STORE

Once harvested, you can store wild rocket in the fridge for 4–5 days.

EAT

Rocket makes a great winter salad and is delicious with generous shavings of Parmesan and a balsamic dressing. The combination of sweet balsamic, salty cheese and peppery leaves is hard to beat.

HOW TO TAKE A CUTTING

Break a large limb off a perennial rocket plant, then grasp a small side shoot and pull it down, separating it from the main shoot.

Make a small hole in damp compost and press the shoot with the trailing 'bark' around it into it. Press the compost down around it.

Rocket is one of the easiest plants to grow and is so prolific that we sometimes think of it as a weed! Rocket makes a great substitute for basil in pesto, and the peppery heat works very well with fresh scallops, too.

SERVES 4

100g (3½oz) pine nuts

12 scallops

plain flour

1 egg, beaten

salt and freshly ground black pepper

2 tablespoons olive oil

FOR THE PESTO

200g (7oz) rocket leaves

100g (3½oz) Parmesan cheese, grated

2 garlic cloves, chopped

50ml (2fl oz) olive oil

15ml (½fl oz) lemon juice

SCALLOPS WITH ROCKET PESTO

First, make the rocket pesto. Place the rocket in a blender and add half the grated Parmesan, the garlic and olive oil. Blitz until it forms a smooth sauce, then add the lemon juice before giving it a final stir. Put into a clean jar and keep in the fridge – it should last for 2–3 weeks.

Next, preheat the oven to 180°C (350°F), Gas Mark 4, then divide the remaining Parmesan into 4 piles on a non-stick baking sheet. Put into the oven for 3 minutes to make crisps.

Meanwhile, crush the pine nuts by placing them in a clean tea-towel and bashing them with a rolling pin, then put the crushed pine nuts on to a plate. Dust the scallops with flour and dip them into the beaten egg. Finally, roll them in the crushed pine nuts and season with salt and pepper. Fry the scallops in the hot olive oil for 2–3 minutes, or until the coating turns golden.

To serve, spoon some pesto on to a plate, place 3 scallops on top and finish with a Parmesan crisp.

METHOD #28

JERUSALEM ARTICHOKES

Jerusalem artichokes are one of the unsung stars of the winter garden. They are a perennial, a relative of the sunflower, and they have fairly ugly tubers that grow profusely and can spread like wildfire. They will also grow very tall, which makes them a great windbreak for an exposed vegetable patch. Jerusalem artichokes are able to grow in a shady or dry site, and their roots will break up clay soils effectively.

WHEN TO PLANT *early to mid spring*

PLANTING DEPTH *15cm (6 inches)*

DISTANCE APART *tubers 30cm (1 foot), rows 1.2–1.5m (4–5 feet)*

WHEN TO HARVEST *early autumn to early spring*

SUCCESSION PLANTING *no*

PLANT

It's very unusual to grow Jerusalem artichokes from seed. They are nearly always planted by using the tubers – source these online or from garden centres. Plant them in early to mid spring. Dig over the soil so that it is soft and well conditioned, and plant the tubers at a depth of 15cm (6 inches) and roughly 30cm (1 foot) apart. Leave at least 1.2–1.5m (4–5 feet) between the rows.

GROW

Jerusalem artichokes are among the very few 'invasive' food plants – they are notoriously difficult to dig up and remove entirely once established. They will reach a height of about 3m (10 feet), so choose their position in your garden carefully. Try planting them near your garden fence, or use them as a windbreak to protect more delicate crops.

You will only need to water Jerusalem artichokes if there is a very serious drought. Cut back the growth at the end of autumn, when the stems and leaves have turned yellow. Leave nothing except small 10cm (4 inch) stumps. It can help to leave the trimmings on top of the plants – this keeps the soil warmer and therefore makes it easier for you to dig them up. Alternatively, mulch the area with a thick layer of straw.

PESTS & DISEASES

Jersusalem artichokes are so hardy and grow so fast that hardly any insects or pests can harm them.

HARVEST

Keep your artichokes in the ground until you are ready to harvest. Dig from at least 30cm (1 foot) away so that you don't skewer any

These plants grow tall!

Artichoke harvest

stray tubers that have spread underground. The great thing about your artichoke crop is that you can keep returning to it over the winter months. If you don't harvest every single one of them, the tubers will regrow next year.

STORE

Leave the artichokes in the ground and cover them with straw mulch if you're in a cold area, or store them in a clamp of moist, but not wet, sand.

EAT

Jerusalem artichokes are excellent in gratins, sautés, stir-fries and soups, and can also be roasted. It's their texture as much as their flavour that makes them special eating — finely diced and added towards the end of the cooking time, they will lend a dish an interesting crunch.

Jerusalem artichokes have a distinctive earthy flavour and a water-chestnut crunch. The boiled artichokes make this a dish with some substance, while the artichoke crisps add a different texture to the mix. You could even add some grated raw artichoke, if you like.

SERVES 4

200g (7oz) Jerusalem artichokes

sunflower oil

a large bunch of rocket leaves

100g (3½ oz) air-dried ham, cut into strips

1 teaspoon capers

a small handful of fresh parsley, chopped

FOR THE MUSTARD DRESSING

juice of 1 lemon

½ teaspoon Dijon mustard

½ teaspoon wholegrain mustard

½ teaspoon white wine vinegar

1-2 tablespoons sunflower oil

1 teaspoon sugar

salt and freshly ground black pepper

FOR THE ARTICHOKE CRISPS

vegetable oil, for deep-frying

2 or 3 Jerusalem artichokes

plain flour

sea salt flakes

zest of 1 lemon

WARM JERUSALEM ARTICHOKE SALAD WITH AIR-DRIED HAM

To make the mustard dressing, mix the lemon juice, mustards, vinegar and sunflower oil in a jug, then add the sugar and some salt and pepper. Set aside.

Bring a large pan of salted water to the boil. Peel and dice the artichokes (excluding the ones needed for the artichoke crisps), then add them to the pan and simmer for 15 minutes.

While the artichokes are cooking, you can make the crisps. Heat some vegetable oil to 190°C (375°F) in a deep-fryer or a large pan. Thinly slice the artichokes and put them on a plate with a sprinkle of flour, sea salt flakes, black pepper and lemon zest. Deep-fry them in the hot oil for 1–2 minutes, until golden brown, then drain on kitchen paper.

When the boiled artichokes are ready, drain them, then put them back into the pan with a drizzle of sunflower oil. Add the rocket leaves, ham, capers and parsley. Heat through for a minute or two, but don't let the rocket wilt too much. Transfer to a serving bowl, toss in the dressing and garnish with the artichoke crisps.

METHOD #29

LEEKS

Leeks are part of the allium family and share some of the characteristics of their cousins -- the garlic and onions of this world. They are easy to grow and delicious. Plus, if you leave a few to flower you can enjoy the beauty of their massive spherical heads: perfect for interplanting in a flower border for some winter visual impact. The best thing about leeks is that they can happily stay in the ground until you want to eat them -- it's essentially pull-to-order shopping!

SOW

Sow seeds in early to mid spring in seed trays or a separate seedbed – sow them thinly, in rows 15cm (6 inches) apart. For bumper crops it's best to improve the growing area by digging in plenty of compost or well-rotted manure in the autumn.

GROW

Leeks are best suited for growing in the open ground, but they can be grown in large, deep containers or raised beds. Transplant the seedlings into their final growing position in early summer, when they are about 20cm (8 inches) long. Take a bunch of young leeks and twist off the top third of the green leaves, leaving you with a higher proportion

WHEN TO SOW *early to mid spring*

SOWING DEPTH *1cm (½ inch)*

DISTANCE APART *rows 15cm (6 inches)*

WHEN TO TRANSPLANT *early summer*

WHEN TO HARVEST *mid autumn to mid spring*

SUCCESSION PLANTING *no*

HARVEST

Use a fork to loosen the ground around the leeks first. Ease the leeks out at the same time that you pull them up. Leeks tend to take a fair bit of cleaning, so rinse them under an outside tap before bringing them into the kitchen.

STORE

It is best to store leeks in the ground. It may take up a bit of space while you get through your crop, but it is so refreshing to let nature do the hard work for you.

EAT

We are suckers for leeks (including a significant amount of the greens) fried slowly in butter. When they are soft, add lemon juice and black pepper – great with a Sunday roast.

of white to green to be planted out. Make a hole and simply drop the plant into it, filling it with water to settle the roots – there is no need to fill it in with soil. The water will gently ease the soil around the roots. You can put a couple of leeks in each hole to grow the same number of slightly smaller ones. Rows of leeks should be about 30cm (1 foot) apart. Weed around the leeks if they are being overcrowded, but generally there is little or no maintenance with leeks, other than harvesting them when you want them.

PESTS & DISEASES

Leek rust can make your leeks look pretty unattractive, but as long as it doesn't take over you will still be able to eat your crop. The best solution is prevention – avoid high humidity levels by leaving enough space between your leeks when you plant them. If it becomes a serious problem, don't grow other alliums on the same patch for a couple of years.

Leeks are very hardy

Leeks are incredibly versatile and make for a fantastic addition to a classic potted crab, introducing a delicious depth and earthiness. Note that potted crab doesn't keep -- but that's fine, as you'll want to eat it all immediately anyway.

SERVES 4

200g (7oz) butter

200g (7oz) leeks, finely chopped

juice of 1 lemon

250g (8oz) cooked crab meat (white and brown)

2 teaspoons chopped fresh tarragon

a pinch of paprika

salt and freshly ground black pepper

POTTED CRAB WITH LEEKS

Melt the butter and pour 4 tablespoons of it into another saucepan. Add the leeks, including some of the green bits, to this second pan. Soften over a medium heat for 5–10 minutes, then add the lemon juice and set aside to cool.

Put the crab meat into a large bowl and add the tarragon, paprika and half the remaining melted butter. Season with salt and pepper and add the cooled leeks.

Spoon the mixture into a jar or ramekin, gently pressing it down to remove any air. Pour the remaining butter on top to seal, then cover and refrigerate until the butter sets. Serve on warm brown toast.

METHOD #30

PARSNIPS

There are not many vegetables that are abundant and at their best from mid autumn all the way through to spring. Before the discovery of the potato, root vegetables such as parsnips were a staple food of northern European peasants. They may not be the most fashionable of vegetables, but parsnips deserve a large plot in your garden, as they are delicious and extremely versatile: they are great roasted, mashed and made into soup – you can even fry them to use as a garnish.

WHEN TO SOW *late winter to early spring*

SOWING DEPTH *1.5cm (¾ inch)*

DISTANCE APART *seeds 15cm (6 inches); rows 30cm (1 foot)*

WHEN TO HARVEST *mid autumn to early spring*

SUCCESSION PLANTING *no*

SOW

The seeds are very light, so sow them on a still day in late winter or early spring. Plant the seeds about 1.5cm (¾ inch) down and cover with a layer of fine soil. The rows should be 30cm (1 foot) apart. Sow batches of 3 seeds every 15cm (6 inches) – this allows for erratic germination and you can thin each batch out so you only have one plant left. Germination is slow, up to a month, so do not give up hope.

Parsnip seedlings don't take well to transplanting, so if you're not planting direct into the garden then sow in degradable pots, or compost-filled toilet rolls, and plant them out in situ.

GROW

Like carrots, parsnips need a stone-free soil that has not been recently manured, but because of the length of their roots it is best to prepare the soil much deeper than for carrots. Some varieties are deliberately developed to give extra long parsnips, but before contemplating growing these, think of the soil and how much preparation you have done.

Healthy parsnip leaves

Apart from a little weeding between the rows, there is little to do in the way of looking after parsnips. In a prolonged dry spell they would obviously appreciate some watering.

PESTS & DISEASES

Listing all the things that can go wrong with parsnips may put you off: celery fly, carrot fly, leaf spot, canker, wireworm, sclerotina rot... But with proper crop rotation and planted near alliums, they will grow quite happily.

HARVEST

Parsnips are best harvested when the green leaves have died back in the autumn. As with most winter crops, it is said they taste better after the first frost, but that is probably to stop you eating your winter vegetable store too early. Use a fork to lift the vegetables you need out of the ground and leave the rest in until required. Be aware that when the foliage has wilted it is sometimes difficult to see exactly where your parsnips are, so pop a twig, or marker stick, into the ground to show the position of the next one to be dug up.

STORE

Although parsnips will survive outside, it is worth storing some in a clamp (see page 121) or in sand in the storeroom for those times when the ground is frozen and digging them up would be difficult.

EAT

Like all root vegetables, parsnips can be roasted, mashed and turned into chips, purées and soups to provide a cheap, filling meal. In fact, you can substitute parsnips in any number of recipes that call for potatoes, celeriac or turnips.

Fresh from the soil

Parnips are sweet-tasting and their texture makes them particularly suitable for soup. Curried parsnips might seem like a strange idea, but trust us, they are delicious.

SERVES 4

750g (1½ lb) parsnips
3 tablespoons vegetable oil
2 tablespoons curry powder
750ml (1¼ pints) chicken or vegetable stock
salt and freshly ground black pepper
vegetable oil, for deep-frying
200ml (7fl oz) cream

CURRIED PARSNIP SOUP

Peel the parsnips and set one of them aside. Cut the rest into 2.5cm (1 inch) chunks. Heat the vegetable oil in a large pan and add the curry powder. Let it cook over a medium heat for a minute to release the flavours, then add the parsnip chunks and cook, stirring, for a couple of minutes.

Add the stock and bring to the boil, then reduce the heat and simmer for 15 minutes. Whizz in a blender or food processor, then taste and season with salt and pepper.

Meanwhile, heat some vegetable oil to 190°C (375°F) in a deep-fryer or a large pan. Finely slice the reserved parsnip and deep-fry the slices for about 45 seconds, or until crisp. Drain on kitchen paper, then sprinkle the crisps with sea salt.

Serve the soup with a swirl of cream on top, and garnish with the parsnip crisps.

KALE

Kale is a traditional brassica that is growing increasingly popular, not only because it is tasty and very good for you, but also because it is incredibly resilient and hardy. Even people who swear they don't have green fingers can grow a decent crop of kale, as there is very little that can kill it. It is also an extremely useful vegetable to grow, as you can have kale available in the garden all winter. Curly kale is a particularly gorgeous-looking plant that makes for a beautiful accompaniment to many a dish.

SOW

From early spring to early summer, sow kale seeds thinly to a depth of 1cm (½ inch), in rows 15cm (6 inches) apart. Thin out the seedlings so that the individual plants are 7cm (3 inches) apart.

GROW

If you have sown your kale in pots, transplant it after about 6–8 weeks, when the seedlings have 5 or 6 true leaves. Moisten the seedling plugs beforehand and leave 30–60cm (1–2 feet) between plants. Water them in really well.

When your kale seedlings are very small they will need protecting with netting or individual cloches – 2 litre (1¾ pint) plastic bottles with the bottom cut off are perfect for popping over young plants. However, once the seedlings have established themselves, kale is a very hardy plant. It is resistant to clubroot and the birds tend to leave it alone.

PESTS & DISEASES

Like all brassicas, kale can suffer from caterpillars: netting plants can be helpful, and it will also keep out other pests, such as aphids and root maggots. We never 'treat' caterpillars, but plant some extra kale instead: the growing season for kale is long, so even if you do lose some of your crop to caterpillars, there is still time for good, un-nibbled leaves to grow. Keeping the pH level of your soil above 6.8 will discourage clubroot.

Protect with netting →

WHEN TO SOW	early spring to early summer
SOWING DEPTH	1 cm (½ inch)
DISTANCE APART	rows 15cm (6 inches), thin seedlings to 7cm (3 inches)
WHEN TO TRANSPLANT	late spring to late summer
WHEN TO HARVEST	early autumn to early spring
SUCCESSION PLANTING	no

HARVEST

From early autumn onwards and all through the winter you can harvest the young tender leaves of your kale. Even once you have picked all the leaves in the crown, delicious side shoots will grow. If you want to treat your kale like a cut-and-come-again crop, start harvesting when the plants are 15cm (6 inches) tall.

STORE

To freeze kale, wash it well, cut up large leaves and remove the toughest stems or 'ribs', then blanch for 2 minutes. Cool and drain well before freezing.

EAT

The smallest leaves are easier to use, but the larger ones have more flavour. Take 5 or 6 large leaves, pull out the main vein and roll them up together into a tight sausage so that you can easily cut them into fine shreds. You can steam shredded kale in a few minutes, and it's great fried with chopped bacon.

Cutting side shoots

We always try to serve our greens fresh and firm rather than boiling them for too long and ending up with a limp leaf. There is no danger of that here: this Asian-style kale has a crispy, crunchy texture that we really enjoy.

SERVES 4

200g (7oz) kale

vegetable oil, for deep-frying

25g (1oz) brown sugar

2 tablespoons sesame seeds

1 tablespoon soy sauce

CRISPY KALE WITH SESAME SEEDS

Heat a few centimetres (an inch or so) of vegetable oil to 180°C (350°F) in a large, lidded pan. Slice the kale very thinly into strips and place directly into the oil. Place the lid on the pan immediately, being very careful not to burn yourself. Remove the kale from the oil with tongs after just 20 seconds and quickly sprinkle with the sugar, sesame seeds and a splash of soy sauce.

INDEX

ACKNOWLEDGEMENTS

Publisher: Stephanie Jackson
Managing Editor: Clare Churly
Copy-editor: Annie Lee
Art Director: Jonathan Christie
Designer: Jaz Bahra
Illustrators: Abigail Read, Charlotte
Strawbridge
Photographer: Nick Pope
Stylist: Alison Clarkson
Kitchen Dogsbody: Jim Tomson
Senior Production Controller: Caroline
Alberti

Picture credits
All photographs are © **Nick Pope** with the
exception of the following: **Alamy** Alison
Thompson 141a; Dave Bevan 168; Richard
Coombs 82; Rob Cousins 103l; Steffen
Hauser/botanikfoto 37r; Westend61 GmbH
132. **Fotolia** Anna Chelnokova 66. **GAP**
Photos Dave Bevan 91a; Juliette Wade 169b;
Mark Winwood 37l; Rob Whitworth 162.
Garden Collection Jonathan Buckley 40,
169a. **Garden World Images** Dave Bevan 99,
159a; Flowerphotos/Jonathan Buckley 141b;
Gary Smith 158; John Swithinbank 163l;
Martin Hughes-Jones 91b, 150. **Getty Images**
Carole Drake 124; Dorling Kindersley 128;
Gary K Smith 121b; Joshua McCullough 121a;
Juliette Wade 29; Lee Avison 110bl; Mark
Bolton 102; Steve Hamilton 28b. **Octopus
Publishing Group** Freia Turland 109br, 147ar,
159b; George Wright 148l; Neil Holmes
110al, 163r. **Photoshot** Biosphoto/Alexandre
Petzold 129b. **Strawbridge Family Archive**
14, 15l & r, 17, 19r, 25al, ar & bl; 26 all, 47l
& r, 48al, ar & bl; 109al & ar; 110br, 147al &
br, 148r. **Thinkstock** Design Pics/The Irish
Image Collection 117b; Hemera 70, 99a;
iStockphoto 33b, 41, 62, 67, 87a 94, 103r,
116, 117a, 132a & b.

Backgrounds: Monica Butnaru/Fotolia;
iStockphoto/Thinkstock

Illustrations: All illustrations are by **Abigail
Read** with the exception of the following:
Charlotte Strawbridge 22, 44, 106, 144.